Failure to Thrive

My Journey to Mental Health

JULIE ANN TOOMEY

Printed in the United States of America

Fourth Printing, 2022

ISBN – 978-1731449085

Thanks to my husband, David, and my good friend, Anna Fry Smith. Without you two, I would still be floundering.

And in loving memory of Lissa Child. May this book save someone from your fate.

Thank you to C. Michelle Jefferies for the inspiration for the book cover. I will pay it forward.

Thanks to all those who helped make this book possible. I'm forever in your debt.

Contents

Introduction

I don't care. I can't care.
The ability to feel is what makes us human. I
know what it is like being without those feelings.
I'm very good at pretending. I can even make
someone think that I understand and empathize.
But I don't. I can't.
I hope that this is a temporary feeling. One that
I will get over sooner rather than later. But I be-
lieve I can understand what would make some-
one look at their life and decide it's not worth
sticking around for. I want to do something with
that knowledge. I want to help people. I want to
make it so that no one ever has to feel this way.

Maybe I do care.

W hy would you continue to feel when all you can feel is pain? How do you keep from turning it off? When the ability to turn off your emotions is so easy—like flipping a switch—why would you leave them on?

In this book, I will share my experiences and take you through my journey to mental wellness. It took me years to get to a point where I can say I have a mental illness. My worldview had to change drastically. It had to be completely reformed. And, as someone who has suffered, I am an advocate for mental health reform in many ways, but mostly in the ways western society talks about mental health. We, as a society, need to understand that depression is more than just sadness, bipolar disorder is more than just changing your mind a lot, and Attention deficit hyperactivity disorder (ADHD) isn't just being unable to sit still. These mental illnesses need to lose the surrounding stigma. Correct information is out there and easily available, but misinformation can lead friends and family members, though well-meaning, to compound the problem. And there is far too much misinformation out there.

If my struggle can help others understand what they're going through and seek the help they need, then it will be worth it. This story is also for the friends and family members of those fighting mental illnesses. Many people don't understand what their loved ones are going through. They don't understand how *real* mental illnesses are, how deeply they can affect the person struggling, and the toll it can take on family. They may not "get" that a mental illness, unfortunately, isn't something you can just fix and that suggestions like "do more service," "think outside yourself," "push yourself to be better," or worst of all "just smile more," while good ideas, don't help as intended, but can instead end up hurting those they love. A mental illness is exactly as it says, an *illness* that is in the brain, and cannot be fixed by simply "sucking it up" or merely making the decision to change.

Mental illnesses are complicated problems with frustratingly complicated solutions. While the most common treatment includes therapy and medication, every person is different. Sometimes therapy is all that's needed, or a medication may be the best solution. Whatever is required, a mental illness isn't something that simply goes away. Sorrow can leave. Moods can change. You can improve your focus. However, when these are signs of a larger complication, the root issue must be addressed, not merely the symptoms.

In order to be allies with those fighting mental illnesses, we need to help rid the world of the stigma surrounding mental illnesses. Conversations about mental illness must be as commonplace as conversations about diabetes or cancer.

I want the world to know what has happened in my life. I will not exaggerate my feelings, but I will not tone them down either. I want you to understand. Because maybe, if you can come to understand, you could really help someone instead of accidentally making it worse. I don't want anyone struggling with mental health to feel like I did, a failure.

CHAPTER ONE

My story begins with a lone child, forced to sit at the dining room table, after everyone else has been excused. I was unable to finish my now cold dinner, even hours after my family had left. It was actually harder once they'd left because there was nothing to distract me from the fact that something disgusting filled my mouth. I gagged and tried to force the flavorless mush down my throat. It didn't work. Gagging again, I continue chewing. Maybe if I mashed it better, it would go down easier. Green beans were, definitely, the grossest thing my young mouth had experienced, and though I had told my parents that multiple times, my mom kept buying them by the can full. I'd watched earlier as she'd dumped the slosh out into a bowl and warmed them in the microwave. I was near tears. I blinked them back, not wanting to show emotion when my dad came in. I wanted the bitter taste out of my mouth, but I couldn't swallow for fear of throwing up. So, I continued chewing, not knowing anything else to do.

"Not done?" my dad asked authoritative-ly, as he walked into the room. I cringed, knowing what was coming next. I swal-lowed as hard as I could, gagging so much that I thought my stomach would come out, but the slop in my mouth went down.

"Can't I be done?" I implored. "My beans are half gone."

"Eat them all," my father stated in a re-signed tone. "Stand up."

I stood, and he sat on my empty chair, pulling me over his knee before spanking me several times. After he got up from my chair, I sat back down on my freshly sore bum. He had repeated that every fifteen minutes since the last person had left the table two hours earlier. I stared at the other half of my beans as he left the room, willing them with all my seven-year-old heart to simply vanish, but it was, of course, in vain. I sighed, picking up another forkful of the slimy vegetables and prayed for the strength to put them in my mouth. It took five more minutes before I could. In a way, I was glad they were cold. Though they tasted worse cold, it wasn't by much and the pungent odor was diminished immensely.

I didn't finish for another hour. Another four spankings. As I finally choked the last bean down my throat, my dad came in to inform me it was time for bed. I'd missed everything, as usual.

This continued to be a common occurrence for some time. It never worked. By the time junior high came around, I wasn't eating any vegetables. They had become the bane of my existence and I couldn't even smell green beans or peas without gagging.

Junior High brought more issues. According to everyone, I was too thin. I looked anorexic. My dad was always telling me that

I didn't eat enough. I needed to eat more. My self-esteem revolved heavily around my weight. Every family activity involved someone mentioning food to me.

"You only eat potatoes." One of my aunts would exclaim while I buried my plate in my favorite food. Potatoes had never tasted bad. They'd never betrayed me.

"Where are your rolls?" One of my uncles would ask with an incredulous grin, thinking he was teasing. I was tearing up, but wouldn't let him see. It wasn't his business what I ate. Why couldn't they all just leave me alone?

But the worst was Thanksgiving with my dad's family. There were always at least thirty people sitting around the table at my grandparents' house. The talking was almost deafening. For some reason, the entire dinner conversation for some seemed to revolve around me and my eating habits. I sat on one side of the long table while my tormentors sat together across from me.

"I see you're eating potatoes again. What else would you be eating?" My uncle's condescending voice boomed at me.

My chest constricted, but I kept quiet. I could see he was eating potatoes too, but I didn't mention it. No mention of the diabetic uncle who doesn't care about *his* diet. Talk about the pot calling the kettle black.

My dad chimed in. "No, she's eating rolls too. See?"

They laughed together. I ate silently, holding back more tears, until I was finally done and full. Then I left the room, finally letting myself cry as I ranted in my journal.

I got some relief at school. Not many of my friends made fun of how I ate, just how I looked, and I could handle that better. I didn't have a ton of friends in junior high, but I also wasn't the least popular person in the school. I had people to sit by at lunchtime. I knew most of the in-jokes. I had a couple of best friends. There was always someone I knew in each of my classes, even if I wasn't specifically friends with them. Still, something was wrong. Though

I was surrounded by people, I was alone. I could almost feel the world passing me by while I stood still, missing everything.

Somehow, among all the friends I had, not one of them could make me feel as welcome as I needed. My desperation shone through and ended up alienating some of the "friends" I already had. The earliest stage of my illness was rearing its ugly head, but I didn't know.

On the first Sunday of the month, members of our church congregation would get up and share experiences with the rest of us. Often, I would hear someone talking about depression (or something like it).

One instance of this was an older lady in the neighborhood who told us how she had struggled with a debilitating depression for a while.

"But I knew that if I had enough faith, God would pull me through and help me overcome it," she stated from the pulpit. "and he did. I no longer feel depressed. I'm alright again."

I sat in our pew, wishing I understood. God took her depression away? Why wouldn't he do that for me? That confused me and kind of hurt. I had faith. I believed in God. I believed He was there. I believed He loved me. That didn't stop the feelings of inadequacy from overwhelming me. It didn't stop the depression from pressing down on me. It didn't stop the inner voices from reminding me of what a horrible person I was.

My mom would tell me to read my scriptures more, do more service, or pray more, every time I commented about my feelings. I poured over my scriptures. I cried during my prayers to God, pleading with Him to take this away, to let me enjoy life. Finally, I began to understand and believe that I wasn't worthy enough for God to heal me. I stopped discussing my feelings about the depression that engulfed me. It was up to me to take care of it, not anyone else.

Nothing changed as I entered high school. I was empty, but I went on with my life. I knew that I didn't deserve anything more, or God would've helped me. I wanted to die. It would be so much easier. I never wanted to do it to myself because I knew that was wrong. I knew there was an after-life. I knew that it would disappoint my ancestors. I knew that it would disappoint God. So I didn't. I couldn't. But that didn't stop me from hoping for a car accident to end it all, or maybe fall asleep and just never wake up. I didn't know they were suicidal thoughts at the time because I never actually considered killing myself. I just wanted an end.

I wanted out of high school. I wanted out of life. I just couldn't handle it anymore. But I had to. I had to handle it. So I did. I knew only one way. I smothered my feelings, buried them, locked them away. I tried my hardest to kill them, but deep down, I knew it wasn't working. The only outlet I allowed myself was my journal. There, I wrote down everything. Every nasty thought I had, every horrible thing I thought about myself and others. No one would ever know.

I learned an unfortunate lesson. Fake it. I faked it with my teachers; I faked it with my family; I faked it with my friends. It continued to get worse. As time went on, many of my friends took my faking as something it wasn't.

The earliest memory I have of this miscommunication was a damaging scene.

"You've got to stop flirting with all the guys in the group. It's getting awkward."

I sat in the corner as the two of them berated me. Feeling trapped and confused, I let them. I wasn't really listening though. What they were saying wasn't true. I wasn't flirting with anyone. I actually had a crush on someone outside the group, so there was no reason to flirt with anyone here.

I stopped hanging out with the lot of them. I didn't know how to communicate any other way, and that was apparently, once again, wrong.

That was my first year of high school. For the next two years, I drifted between groups, never belonging, never feeling accepted. I would sit with a crowd in a corner and not talk to anyone. I would sit with the guy I liked and his friends. They were inclusive and kind, so even though Brian didn't share my feelings, they allowed me to join them.

Veronica was one that would mock me for my weight. I was too thin, I was too small. She couldn't believe that I could go without wearing a bra. Her small group was one I visited a lot. She and Liv had been friends of mine since elementary school. The two friends I knew the best. I wanted to be accepted so desperately that any acknowledgment was better than nothing. But I didn't feel like I deserved any acceptance. Being on the outside was my life, what I was made for. I almost welcomed the ridicule.

There were times when the mental anguish was apparently not enough. I also endured a lot of physical discomfort during this time. Doubling over in pain would be a weekly occurrence for a while as it felt like a ball of agony would radiate from my stomach. I wondered if it was my appendix or my gallbladder. I wondered so many things, but we found nothing. I would get nauseated and feel sick. A friend once asked me if I was pregnant. That actually hurt, because although I'm fairly certain he was joking, this was during my junior year of high school. I was a good little Christian girl who'd never even kissed a guy.

My grades were horrible. My attendance was great simply because it had been so solidly drilled into me, "You go to school." There wasn't a question. I was mocked by so many and disliked by others, something that was now normal for me, that it made school a nightmare for me. But, it was fact. All the things people said about me were obviously true because so many people were saying them.

My senior year I spent some time at an alternative school doing packets. I'd failed enough classes that I wasn't going to graduate. The depression was so intense that I hadn't been able to focus. In many ways, I wish I could have done all my schooling through packets. I was able to do it at my own pace and I got them done almost perfectly, and quickly too. I learned more from those three packets than I had in the months of classes they were meant for. I struggled and pushed myself harder than I had before, finally earning decent grades my senior year because my parents had told me that I wouldn't get my driver's license if I didn't. That threat wasn't really the tipping point for me, but a reminder that I needed to find a tipping point of some kind. The grades still weren't amazing, but it was sufficient for my parents. With most of my friends not really wanting anything to do with me, I threw myself into my school work and did better. I was still as depressed as ever though.

The moment I graduated, I thought that my troubles were behind me. I never had to endure school again. I didn't have to see any of those people ever again. I wouldn't have to feel like a useless waste of space.

What I learned:

- High School is hard. It's even harder if you don't let people in.

- Depression does exist, even when people in your life say otherwise. Let yourself admit to it and let someone help you with it.

- Depression can warp your view and your friends might still be your friends, even when it seems like they aren't.

Actions You Can Take:

- Talk to someone. Let them know that you're hurting. Even if it's just online to a support group about mental illness, or an online friend you don't know well, talk.

- Talk to your friends. Let them know you're hurting. Statistically speaking, at least one of your friends is affected by a mental illness, is hurting, and feels alone.

CHAPTER TWO

With high school over, I needed to finally acquire a full-time job. I'd done odd jobs since Junior High for my mom's office, but I never had a real job with a real paycheck. After graduation, I went and applied for as many places as I could find. I had no idea what I was doing, but I wrote up my nearly empty resume with my mom's help and started searching. It wasn't surprising that it took me months to find anything. I couldn't allow myself to get discouraged though. I was excited to be in the real world. I knew this would fix my problems. Everything would be better; it would be different. I no longer had to deal with school and all its drama.

I was able to secure a job at a local thrift store, which sounded really cool during the interview. It was nothing like I expected. Though my coworkers were adults, they didn't act like it. The petty power struggles and popularity contests should have been behind us. But in reality, they started with my manager. He didn't help any of the employees and strutted around the store aimlessly unless someone higher up was there. Then he acted like he cared, hopping on a register, answering our questions, etc. His worst antics brought many to tears, including myself. It always felt that, for some unknown reason, he hated me. He seemed to go out his way to belittle me and impose excess work on me. The constant ridicule I received, once again, confirmed that I was a waste, and no one cared about me.

I tried hard to be who I was "supposed" to be, whatever that meant. I worked hard and did what my manager ordered me to do, suck it up. I ended up quitting eight months later. I was a little surprised that I lasted that long. That place helped me realize that I needed to go back to school. I wanted more out of life than constant repetitive work.

I was still having so many health problems and I couldn't figure out what was causing them. We'd had my appendix and my gall bladder both checked. The doctors couldn't find anything wrong. My dad suggested many times that it was all in my head. Until one day he suggested something different.

"You know," my dad stated, "you might have celiac disease."

I had no idea what that was, but I latched onto it.

"I might. What is it?"

"It's when your body can't handle any gluten in your system. Here, why don't you use my computer? You can research it."

I looked it up and learned all I could about it. That day, I started on a gluten-free diet.

A lot of my pain went away. This was what was wrong with me. I knew it. I couldn't believe the answer had been so simple. Change my diet. It cut out most of my favorite foods, but if it meant no more pain,

I would handle it. Besides, I found great gluten-free recipes for some of those foods, anyway.

A year after I graduated I took the ACT and applied for Snow College—a little college in a tiny town in Southern Utah. I saved up some money from a call center job that I'd had for a few months before college. Finally, I headed down with no car, no friends, and no clue what I wanted to study. But when I finally clambered into a car filled with my stuff, I was anxious as I waited for my mom to join me.

"Mom! We're going to be late!"

"It's fine. I'm coming."

I drummed my fingers as silently as I could on my leg. In a way, I was glad my mom didn't like small talk, but this drive seemed to be taking forever. I tried to distract myself by pondering what it would be like down there. No parents to tell me when and where to go. I hoped I'd make friends. I hoped that I would be able to succeed. It had been a year since I'd been in school and I hadn't done that well then. But this time would be different. This time would be better.

When we arrived, I found the apartment and picked up my key from the landlady. Suddenly I was insecure. Who would my roommates be? Would they think me weird? What would they be like? I walked into the apartment only to find it empty and decided those questions would have to be answered later. I dumped my stuff on the one empty bed left and went back outside to help my mom grab the rest of my clothes and items for my room.

It felt like I'd successfully run away from my problems. But I still didn't have that feeling of home. There was still a tingle in my brain; a depression that still lingered in the background. But I refused to acknowledge it. At school I felt okay. I felt like I could function. I was meeting new people and making friends. I even felt happy. I had the confidence to do something I'd never done: I taught myself college algebra out of the book after my teacher proved to be inept. It was the only "A" I earned that semester.

At home, I was alone. My roommates tried to act like my parents, constantly berating me for little things. They'd have parties into the early hours of the morning, even when school was the next day. I bought earplugs, but they only barely kept the sound quiet enough to sleep.

I joined the archery club and loved it. I learned various weapons—longbows, knives, hatchets, and my favorite, the compound bow—which was fascinating and somehow calming. The easy draw of the compound bow string through the pulleys made it different from the long bows and I was able to aim with it better. I always left archery club less stressed than I'd entered.

The archery club president had a slew of other weapons, including katanas and guns. I was able to hold those and semi-practice with them, though not to the extent of the bows. I was finally getting out of my sheltered little life, learning more about the world, and I *loved* it! Whenever I became frustrated, I was able to pull out the foam nunchakus that I had borrowed from the archery club president and practice with them. That usually calmed me down without the need to yell at anyone.

I arrived home for the summer and started back up at the call center. For some reason, they moved me from the supervisor position that I enjoyed, to a tiny cubicle in a dark room without so much as a warning. I was doing data entry while sitting at a desk and interacting with no one. Everything I'd like about the job the previous summer was gone. No friends, no light, no communication with anyone. When I asked about my old position, I was promptly booted out. Fired without a second thought. With no income, I didn't have the money to go back to college to finish my degree. What had happened? I thought I had put this drama and insanity behind me. I thought I was done being fired from jobs. From quitting jobs. From failing at life.

I shut down for a short while. I tried and tried to come out of it, to push myself to be better. I tried to study more, pray harder. Isn't that what they tell you to do? I tried, but I was trapped inside myself. There were times when I couldn't climb out of bed and times when I would watch TV for thirty-six hours straight. I couldn't focus. When I watched that much TV, I didn't even feel tired at the end of it. The only reason I slept was because logically, I knew I needed sleep. I was spiraling, and I didn't know how to stop. My motivation to do anything was at another low.

It took a while, a lot of soul searching, and quite a few lectures from my mom, but I found another job, and lost it soon after. I started a third job and lost it too. My ability to focus was impaired, and I hated everything I had to do. I carried on a continual round of finding and losing, or quitting, jobs in a dizzying whirl. I'd either get fired because I couldn't focus, or quit because I hated the job. The longest I'd ever held down a job was nine months at a craft store. I was trying. I was trying so hard and was so desperate for *something*, some clarity or enjoyment. It always seemed barely out of reach.

I started going to a church ward, or congregation, of single adults around my age, where my best friend attended. I met amazing people in that ward, and was, for the first time in a really long time, asked on a date. His name was Jeff.

At the end of the date, Jeff leaned in and I hugged him. He pulled back with a little furrow in his brow. "Maybe next time, then?"

"Yeah," I said, unsure as to what he was referring. It wasn't until I closed the door to my bedroom and started getting ready for bed that I realized he'd tried to kiss me. I'd missed my *first kiss*!

The next night we were watching a television show and suddenly Jeff moved in on me and his lips were on mine. He was kissing me! I had no idea what to do, so I tried to simply follow his lead. As I left that night, I was on cloud nine. But confused. What about the guy I still had a crush on? What about Brian?

I tried to forget him and started dating Jeff. It didn't take long—less than a week—for me to realize that he wasn't what I wanted. I didn't know what was happening. I had no idea what to do in a relationship. When he tried to hold my hand, I thought he was trying to take my phone and snatched it away. It was awkward and weird. *I* was awkward and weird. I broke up with him a week after our first kiss and moved on to other things. I decided that I needed to figure out my life. I thought about going on a mission for my church. God had once told me that I needed to, back when He was talking to me, but that was a year-and-a-half long commitment. I wasn't sure if I was ready for that. I certainly didn't have the money for it.

Before I could make that decision, I needed to talk to Brian. I made him a CD with a few songs on it and then talked to him after church one day.

"So, as you could probably tell from the CD, I have feelings for you."

He nodded, looking decidedly uncomfortable. "I think of you as a friend. A good friend, but just a friend nonetheless."

I nodded as well. I had seen this coming, honestly. Deep down, I knew I didn't deserve him. Why would God give me someone like him anyway? He knew I wasn't worthy of Brian.

"I just needed you to know."

I left the room, trying not to cry.

By the time I made the decision to turn my missionary paperwork in, I'd already applied to go back to Snow College for the summer. I thought about not going. I thought about taking a leave of absence. I contemplated hard. But I had already paid for it, so there wasn't any backing out, no matter what I wanted.

I went. I was still on my special diet for celiac disease and it continued to make life hard for me. The allure of it had worn off and now it was simply something I had to do. The few times I cheated I felt nothing. No pain, no problems. It made me question if that was really my issue, but I didn't know and I couldn't tell. The pain was still there but it seemed random, with no correlation to what I ate.

I took really cool classes that summer that I enjoyed immensely, but I hated how I felt the whole time. Human anatomy, while normally interesting and fascinating, was now dull and boring. I made no friends. I had no roommates. The store where I worked closed halfway through the summer, leaving me alone, except for at church where I didn't feel comfortable like I had with my old congregation. I'd never been as depressed as I was then. I felt I was supposed to be on my mission already; the pull was overwhelming. I wrote in my journal how I couldn't explain the way I felt. I thought about telling my mom what I was feeling, but I couldn't explain because I didn't understand it myself. No one else could possibly understand it if I couldn't, so I didn't even see the point in trying.

I didn't have the words to explain that it felt like there were two different people inside of me. It was almost like I was constantly arguing with myself about what I should do, what I should be. I couldn't figure out who was going to win. I couldn't even figure out what they were arguing about sometimes. I knew no one could help me. No one could understand.

In the midst of the summer, I ended up going to a family doctor down near the college and figured out something really was wrong. Someone finally believed that I was in immense pain and took the time to look for the problem. The ultrasound tech searched my gallbladder until she found tiny stones—enough to at least make the doctors pause. So, after years of pain, I was officially diagnosed with gallstones and told I needed to have my gallbladder removed. The doctors told me that my gallbladder had been not only functioning on a lower level than normal, but was the wrong color! Whereas it should have been green, mine was white. It was a very good thing they had removed it.

For a while, I wondered if God was helping me, but I realized once again that I simply wasn't good enough. I was going to church every week, reading my scriptures every day, praying morning and night, and writing in my journal daily. Obviously, this wasn't enough. I wasn't feeling any better psychologically. I began to question God's love for me. Could God love me and allow me to feel this way? How could God care about me and not answer my plea?

I finally finished school and started a new job as I worked on my mission application and waited for my call to come. Finally, one day, my mom called with news that it had arrived.

I drove home as fast as I could without breaking any laws. Questions started flying through my mind as furiously as the butterflies were in my stomach. Where would I be going? Would I learn a new language? What kind of culture would there be there? What kind of history? My mind conjured up many images of potential mission calls: Bolivia, Russia, Alaska, South Africa. Would I really be able to handle this as my friends assured me I could?

I was frustrated as the cars in front of me moved at what seemed to be a snail's pace. I had a life-changing envelope lying on my bed and they were all acting as though it were just another Wednesday. I calmed myself by saying aloud that they were probably doing me a favor as, in my haste to find out where I was going, I would probably speed and end up getting pulled over.

I finally pulled up in front of my house, threw the car in park, turned it off, pushed open my door, and raced inside. As I rounded the corner to go down the stairs to my room, I was going so fast that I had to brace myself against the wall with my hand to avoid crashing. I took the maze of the basement at a higher speed than ever before, until at last, I entered my room and saw the beautiful, mundane whiteness of the envelope.

It seemed to stare at me, waiting to be opened, and was almost deceptive. On the outside, by looking at it, no one would think it was anything special. But the letter that was inside that envelope would tell me when and where eighteen months of my life would be spent. A calm washed over me as I pulled out the knife I carried in my back pocket for opening boxes at work, and slashed open the top of the envelope. I tried not to see my fate until I had it completely open and could take the letter out.

Dear Sister Bateman,
You are hereby called to serve as a missionary of the Church of Jesus Christ of Latter-day Saints. You will serve in the Pennsylvania, Harrisburg Mission. It is estimated that you will serve for eighteen months.

I stopped reading. Pennsylvania! Wow! There was amazing church and American history there, not to mention my own family history. It would be so cool to serve there. I had always wanted to go back east and now, here was my chance. No, I wouldn't be sightseeing, but I might have that chance on the occasional break day. I continued reading.

You should report to the Missionary Training Center in Provo, Utah on Wednesday 2 January 2008. You will prepare to teach the gospel in the English language. Your mission president may modify. . .

Oh, Wow. That was less than two months away! There was so much to do! The excitement washed back over me and I suddenly had to tell someone. I turned and ran out of my room to go tell my mom upstairs.

What I learned:

- Mental illnesses can actually show up as bodily problems. I fully believe that my stomach problems came from the fact that I was unmedicated, but had a mental illness.

- Mental illnesses can be very scary. But you'll never outrun them. They must be faced head on.

Actions You Can Take:

- Make sure you go to the doctor for your annual physical. Talk to him or her about anything that's going on. They can often help if you're feeling depressed, anxious, or something else. They won't judge you. They're used to seeing patients with problems. They'll be happy that you're asking for help! And it's okay to need help.

Chapter Three

In January of 2008, I entered the Missionary Training Center (MTC) in Provo, Utah. I was excited and hopeful. Walking away from my family for the last time, I didn't even look back. This was where God wanted me and I was determined to do what He wanted. I knew that this intense sorrow would go away if I did this.

Through the entire two and a half weeks of my field training, however, depression pounded down on me. Everyone was assigned a work companion for the short time they were in the MTC. My companion and I clashed often about the rather strict missionary rules. We spent more time arguing than we did studying. I continued to hide my despair. I quickly discovered, to my dismay, that I hated it there. I wanted to go home. Why wasn't the sorrow subsiding? Why wasn't I happy? My whole experience was painted with a disgusting shade of depression that left me hating every minute.

While I didn't cry myself to sleep most nights, I felt like it every night. One night, as I knelt on my bed, so tempted to ask God to send me home, I instead found myself asking if he loved me. Suddenly I was overwhelmed, engulfed by an intense understanding, a deep abiding peace. I knew God couldn't lie. I knew this was a yes. That didn't make it easy. I still despised being there. That short burst of calm seemed to fade. I held on to it as tightly as I could, I needed this, but it was like water in my hands. The more desperately I held, the more it slipped away from me.

"We shouldn't be playing that music, Sister."

I was playing an album that I had specifically brought because it was spiritually uplifting. Seriously, Josh Groban had to be okay to listen to.

"What do you mean?"

"It's not done by the church."

"No, but it's uplifting and helps me feel the Spirit. I like it."

"We still shouldn't be playing it." She replied loudly. Our roommates looked over at us.

"Then leave the room if you don't like it."

"I can't leave the room. You're here so I have to be here."

I groaned. This was one of those things that Sister Jenson and I had argued about non-stop.

Deciding it wasn't worth it to argue over her arbitrary rules, I turned the music off and flopped onto my bed. Why was I here again?

One of the speakers at a devotional we had every Sunday told us that God had called us to this place to be missionaries; He wouldn't end our service prematurely. I wouldn't be called home early. That stuck with me. It made me feel guilty about my intense desire to go home. I decided that no matter what happened, I couldn't, I wouldn't, go home early. I would do everything in my power to find a way to be happy, to bury the depression, to bury everything. All of my sadness, my annoyance, my hatred of where I was, were stamped down and hidden deep inside. I had the will, there must be a way.

Because my mission companion and I were fighting so frequently, I was forced to talk to a therapist for the first time in my life. Our conversations were empty. I'd always known that therapy was for the weak. Those too feeble minded to figure it all out themselves. So, I lied my way through it. If he really knew what was going on in my brain, I knew that he would send me home early and I'd already decided that wasn't an option. I couldn't go home early. How disgraced and unworthy would that make me? Heavenly Father would strengthen me. He had to. I knew he would. I would stay out the whole eighteen months.

It was time to fly out to the mission area, my field training was over. I'd spend the next eighteen months doing what I was supposed to do and I was looking forward to it. I think. Maybe not. I knew it was what God wanted. But I wanted to run. I wanted to hide. I was at war with myself, jumping between the desire to be God's instrument and selfishly wanting nothing of the kind. When we arrived, I was assigned a different companion and a work region. We were sent to Hershey, Pennsylvania. My new companion was a great person but she definitely didn't mesh well with my personality. She seemed to be one who truly loved it there. I was simply determined to be the person that God wanted me to be. I worked diligently, hiding my annoyance with the whole situation. I hid that I wanted to curl up in a ball on my bed and cry. Was it homesickness? Or was it more?

The first night there, as soon as we arrived at my new home, I set my stuff in the room and asked what the plan was for the night.

My companion was, understandably, very excited about my "go-to" attitude, and so we headed out to an appointment she had set for us. He was an amazing man from China who had already decided to be baptized. He even had a date chosen and was very excited. His excitement made me wonder about my own lack of enthusiasm. His accent made prayers difficult to understand, but I could tell he felt God's love. I kept pushing myself, hoping that meeting more people like this, and learning as much as I could, would cure me. It would make me happy. It would show me how.

Those first six weeks were mentally exhausting. My companion wanted to learn more about me than I was ready to share.

"What are you thinking about Sister Bateman?"

I came out of my scenery-induced coma to look at her. "Nothing."

She let out a groan of frustration. "You can't be thinking of nothing. Come on. What are you thinking about?"

I couldn't help but wonder why she wanted to know so badly. Whatever the reason, I didn't have an answer for her. I had literally had nothing on my mind. It was my one reprieve from the hell I experienced every day.

"Nothing," I repeated forcefully. This intrusion wasn't welcome. Even if I had something on my mind, it was none of her business.

Two weeks after I arrived, on my birthday, I realized that I had forgotten frosting for a cake that I had made and we didn't have time to stop and buy any. I told my mission companion that if God was okay with me having frosting for my birthday, He'd provide it somehow. I still held on to that belief, that he cared. It had to be true.

The family we had dinner with that night knew it was my birthday and made a chocolate cake. Somehow, the wife told me, they had made twice as much frosting as needed. When they asked if we wanted it, I turned and smirked at my mission companion who was staring at me with wide eyes. I needed that reassurance, that God cared for me even with small things. That was no longer in question.

Still, I kept up the rest of the facade. I needed to prove to everyone that this was where I belonged. I needed to prove to myself that this was where I belonged. Because God called me here and He wouldn't call me home prematurely. I continued strong. I don't think I had ever buried my feelings nearly as well as I did in those first six weeks. It was probably the most trying time of my mission.

I found it easier to relate to my next mission companion. She was going home soon and was so excited. It was a little less challenging to work with her because we somewhat understood each other. I didn't want to be there; she didn't want to be there. We continued to serve faithfully, but it was a lot more pleasant than my first six weeks. We'd talk every day about clean comedians. She would quote her favorite ones while we were walking around knocking doors. We spent a lot of time laughing together.

When she returned home, I was assigned yet another mission companion. She had converted to the Church later in life. That was a new experience for me. I didn't know very many converts. I had grown up sheltered in Utah Valley. We talked a lot, and I learned about her experience in making the decision to be baptized.

Since it was getting warmer, she and I started biking around the city. She hadn't biked much during her mission, but that didn't stop her from pushing herself. She inspired herself by murmuring encouraging words while pedaling, especially when going uphill. I believe the exercise really helped my depression because I was feeling somewhat better. Whether it was God blessing me or something else, I was doing what I needed to do and I was, almost, happy. My mission companion's humor and her enjoyment of life really helped. I was able to laugh. I was able to smile. She never seemed depressed. She never seemed to become discouraged. She was truly an inspiration to me.

After six weeks with that companion, I was transferred to a new area in Lititz and was assigned a new mission companion,

Sister Nelson. After two months, she informed me that I was very difficult to love. The reason? I didn't love myself. That was tough to hear. I was trying so hard to do all the right things and here was this woman, whom I considered a friend, telling me that I was hard to love.

She told me about her life, the things she had gone through, and the problems she had overcome. I came to realize that she could relate to me, and I to her. She understood a little of what I was going through and could give me valuable advice. She taught me that therapy wasn't something to be ashamed of or to look down on people for. That therapy wasn't for the weak-minded, but for those who needed help figuring things out and were willing to ask. She told me that everyone needs help figuring things out at some point in their lives. I listened. Perhaps it was because I desperately needed something to hold onto, something to show me that I would end up being ok. She helped me figure out that I really did need help. I decided I would wait until I went home. That would be soon enough. I thought about talking to the mission therapist but kept putting it off. It never seemed to be the right time. I was fine for now. Besides, he might send me home early.

A short time later, I sat there, sobbing, clutching the phone in one hand as the other covered my eyes in a futile attempt to stop the stream of tears pouring from them. I knew it was an overreaction. Grown women don't curl up in the back of a closet like a blubbering child. But that didn't stop me.

The problem had started earlier that day when my mission companion told me that we couldn't leave the apartment until I ate something. I wasn't hungry, so I told her that I'd eat when we came back tonight. Apparently, that hadn't been good enough.

"Eat something, or we aren't leaving."

"I'm not hungry. I told you, I'll eat when we get back. I can't eat when I'm not hungry."

"You haven't had any lunch. You have to eat something."

I rolled my eyes. I hardly ever ate lunch. Six pancakes for breakfast went a long way.

"I'm fine. Now can we go?"

That's when she dropped the proverbial bomb.

"No. I've been told to look after you and make sure you're eating. So, eat something!"

My jaw dropped as flashbacks of meals with my father flew through my mind. Memories of sitting at the table for hours, being told that I couldn't leave until I ate whatever gag-worthy food had been placed on my plate. My life was suddenly on repeat. Still trapped, I hadn't really escaped.

Tears filled my eyes as I grabbed the shared cell phone and stomped to the closet in the extra bedroom where my clothes hung and curled up into a ball. Then I called the only person who could have asked Sister Nelson to spy on and control me—the mission president's wife. While the mission president was in charge of the missionaries' spiritual and logistical concerns, it fell to his wife to care for our physical and emotional needs. It could only be her.

"I need you to tell Sister Nelson to please not watch my food intake. I'm twenty-two years old. I've taken a nutrition class in school. Twice. What I choose to eat or not eat, when I choose to eat or not eat, should be entirely up to me."

The power of my words caused my tears to start flowing and it felt like all the mental and emotional stress I'd been hiding and fighting against for the last eight years broke me.

"I just need it to stop. I need to stop being checked up on. I need to be able to care for myself without someone looking over my shoulder." I was babbling into the phone, trying my hardest to keep my voice level down so Sister Hansen couldn't tell how much I was sobbing. I knew the mission president's wife could tell anyway, but I had to try.

Her voice was calm. "I'm sorry; I didn't realize that you felt that way. I'm only concerned about your eating habits."

I groaned. Once again, everyone was concerned with my eating habits. For the past twenty-two years that had been all I'd ever heard - "I'm concerned about your eating habits." I was an adult living away from home, and not for the first time. I had just learned that my new mission companion had been told to spy on me. I wondered briefly if previous ones had been given the same instructions. I thought I'd gotten away from people trying to parent and control me.

She couldn't possibly know what I meant. I was still figuring it out myself. But at this moment, I reached a clarity that had never been available to me before this moment. I realized that I was so deep into this pit of despair that I couldn't see any hope. There was no joy – only fleeting moments of happiness that came and went in the blink of an eye. Happiness was such a foreign concept that its absence was something that I never questioned. All I felt was lost. I knew something was wrong. Sister Nelson had pointed that out many times, but for the first time, I realized for myself that something desperately needed to change.

Sister Hansen invited us to their home so that I could talk to President Hansen in person. She then asked to speak to my companion, who was now standing just outside the closet. I'm sure that Sister Nelson thought I was complaining about her—trying to get her in trouble. I wasn't, but I couldn't even look at her as I reached up and handed her the phone. What right did they have to decide if I could care for myself? As I sulked in my room, I realized the original request had probably come from my parents.

On the way to the Hansens', I barely registered the beautiful trees and green Pennsylvanian scenery passing by; my heart wasn't paying attention to what normally gave me comfort. A part of my brain had gone blissfully blank while another part frantically tried to figure out what might happen to me. How could I tell the leader of my mission that I didn't want to be there? How could I tell him that I wanted to go home?

Many people would accuse me of disobeying God. Of going against His teachings. President Hansen was the sweetest man I knew, but still, I was concerned.

Words flew through my mind. The same words that had been there nearly every day since I began those two weeks at the Missionary Training Center. "You were called here by a prophet of God; you're not going to be called home prematurely." How I wish I had never heard that stupid talk. As that thought crossed my mind, I berated myself. That talk was given by a member of the Quorum of the Seventy, a group of higher up leaders in the Church. His talk shouldn't be referred to as "stupid". But I couldn't change how I felt. Those words were making my life absolute hell. I knew that the man who said them was called of God. That, of course, only made it worse. I knew I was called to this place. I knew God wanted me here. The desire to go home didn't belong inside me. But I had tried for seven long months—nearly half of the normal year-and-a-half mission—to stamp it down, to bury it, to not let it advertise its hatred for my mission. Obviously, it was stronger than I was.

I couldn't stop a sigh when we pulled into the neighborhood and I saw the mission home in front of us. Sister Nelson carefully pulled the car into the driveway and I sat there, partly relieved at finally being there, and part frustrated at being there at all.

As we walked into the house, Sister Hansen greeted us both with big hugs and President Hansen shook our hands, smiling his trademark smile. I had never seen him without it. I wondered what would happen after he heard what I had to say. What could I say? This shouldn't have happened in the first place.

Sister Nelson stayed back with Sister Hansen as I followed President Hansen into his office and he shut the door behind us. I was apprehensive as I sat in the chair across from him. The thoughts I'd had in the car came rushing back. How was I supposed to explain to him how I felt? If I told him I wanted to go home, I knew he would try to talk me out of it. I wasn't supposed to go home. Those were the words that had haunted me daily. So why did I feel like that was exactly what was happening? I didn't want to tell him how I felt, but I knew I had to. Something needed to happen, and I didn't know what it was, but I couldn't go on this way. His calling allowed him to receive revelation for those he was responsible for, for me. Perhaps he could receive the clarity that was eluding me.

"Sister Bateman, do you mind if we start with a prayer?"

I shook my head. Of course, I didn't mind. I needed guidance and only God could give me that.

President Hansen said a quick prayer asking for help to figure out what I needed. After he closed, I remained silent. I had no idea what to say. So many thoughts were racing through my head that I couldn't focus on one alone.

"What's on your mind, Sister?"

I shook my head and let out a tiny breath of laughter. "I don't know. I just, I can't do this." I started crying. "I want to go home."

I let my head drop even more, dreading his reaction.

"Okay." His calm voice washed over me. I looked up at him.

"It's okay for you to go home, Sister Bateman. And I think you do need to go home. You're obviously having problems. We can make sure you receive the help you need. As a sister missionary, it won't be hard to get you approved to go."

I stared at him, stunned. It was okay for me to go home? I could leave? That was allowed? The weight and crushing pain that had been building over the past seven months suddenly lifted off of me and I was at a loss for words.

"Thank you."

"You're welcome. Was there anything else you needed, Sister? I have a feeling that's not all that's on your mind."

Our talk turned into a two-hour long conversation that seemed more like a therapy session. This time, I opened up. By the end of it, President Hansen told me that he would look into when I could be sent home and asked me to continue praying about the decision. The peace I felt, however, told me that it was the right choice. But I promised that I would continue to pray. I was planning on it anyway.

A week later we went to Zone Conference, a regional meeting that happened once every six weeks for all the missionaries there. It was filled with lessons and guidance on how to better serve the people of Pennsylvania and encouragement in the work. God's love filled my heart as I heard words from his servants.

This is where I belong, I thought, right here.

I knew I still couldn't stay out the whole time, but maybe one more transfer, just six more weeks. I could do that. That wouldn't be hard. Sister Nelson was going to be transferred to a different area soon, she'd been here for 9 months already, and Sister Dahlia was almost brand new. She'd joined us because of my emotional state and the possibility of me going home. I could help her learn the area and meet the people. I would be the senior companion for the first time on my mission. I'd be in charge. That would be nice. So many things were running through my mind that I could barely keep up, but, by the end of the day, as the conference was ending, I felt that I had made my decision. Six more weeks, then I'd leave. Just six more weeks.

I felt content as we headed home. I felt like I'd be okay. I discussed my thoughts with my two mission companions and they agreed with me. It was a good plan.

The next day was whiplash. The worst day I'd had since arriving in Pennsylvania. I felt more lethargic than I ever had in my entire life. Nothing felt wrong physically, but it was as though every thought I had was having to break through a wall of mud to reach my consciousness. After our morning scripture study, when we were supposed to go out and teach people, I couldn't. I told Sisters Nelson and Dahlia that I'd wake up shortly, I was sorry, but there was no way I'd be able to function if I went out like that. I felt bad since we had a few appointments that day, but my brain was so foggy that I couldn't even remember who they were with.

I was in and out of it all day. Every time I awoke, my brain seemed determined to hold me down. I couldn't explain it. I felt completely miserable. Finally, at the end of the day, I knelt beside my bed, pleading with the Lord.

"Please just let me go home. I don't think I can do this. I just want to go home."

Immediately my mind cleared, and I heard a voice clearly say "okay".

I paused. "Okay?" I asked. "I can really go?"

My Heavenly Father answered me as strongly as I'd ever received an answer before. "Go home. Get the help you need. Come back when you're ready."

"If I go home, I'm not coming back."

"We'll see." I could hear the love in His voice and knew this was my answer. I was going home. More importantly, I was going home soon. The relief I felt was almost indescribable.

Relief was quickly pushed away by the shame of the decision. Guilt and disgrace flooded me. I was going home early.

What I Learned:

- You'll only let others love you as much as you love yourself. If you don't see yourself as worth it, it's difficult to believe others' love for you.

- God has a hand in your life. He'll pull you up, even when it's hard to understand why.

Actions You Can Take:

- Find something worth living for. Do you believe in a higher power? Whatever you can believe in, believe in it, it will make it easier.

- Try not to let yourself get to the point where you break down. If you find yourself floundering, as I did while I was on my mission, seek help immediately. Tell someone who can find you that help. It's easier to row the boat to shore when it's not already sinking.

Chapter Four

I sighed as I leaned against the window and watched the ground slowly pass by, miles below me. My mission hadn't gone as it was supposed to. It was supposed to be the best thing to ever happen to me. It was supposed to have lasted a year and a half. It was supposed to make me happier and more mature.

And yet, I found myself sitting on a plane, headed home from the mission I hated, seven and a half months after it began. My brain was at war with itself; one side was fighting for guilt, the other side basking in relief. Both God and President Hansen told me it was okay, but that was hard to swallow.

I was the only one of my siblings to come home early. Everyone would wonder why

I couldn't cut it, why I was coming home. Utah Valley isn't a place to mess up and I'd messed up badly. Only screw-ups and sinners came home from their missions early. Which one would my friends and family assume I was? I felt as though I had a giant red F emblazoned on my shirt for the world to see.

I wondered briefly if anyone at home would even recognize me. The depression was causing me to slip even more into a shell that was quickly becoming my home, my sanctuary, my prison. The real world seemed like a distant memory, a dream that I had mixed into the truth.

It felt weird to be leaving. It felt as though I was leaving home and heading to it at the same time. I wondered how long it would be until I could shake this lost feeling that had been following me around.

Most of the trip was a blur. I waited in the Cincinnati airport for my connecting flight and then watched a movie for the rest of the trip home. The man sitting next to me tried to strike up a conversation, but eventually gave up when he realized that I just couldn't do it. I felt bad about that. The badge on my shirt labeled me as a missionary. I should have been upbeat and friendly. I should have been talking to everyone about the gospel, shouting the good news from the rooftops and telling everyone that it made me so incredibly happy. But I couldn't. It wasn't that I didn't want to talk to anyone. Rather the disconnection I felt with the world was so strong that the man beside me didn't even seem real.

The plane finally set down in the Salt Lake City airport and everyone slowly filed off. Waiting my turn, I followed the man that had been sitting next to me and slowly made my way through the airport to the pick-up area. I smiled tiredly at the sight of my family. Everyone had made it. All five of my siblings, and their families, stood waiting. My parents stood a little in front of the group. All of their eyes were on me.

When I made it to the end of the escalator, I met my mom halfway and gave her a hug. It had been an unwritten rule that

Mom always gets the first hug. When Adam, my oldest brother, got home he had actually brushed past my younger brother, Lucas, to hug my mom first. Ever since then that's the way it was.

Dad was second. I got swept up into the bear hug that he always gave and relaxed into his embrace. Memories of him were part of why I broke down and had to come home. But during the session with my Mission President, I'd realized why he'd done those things and had forgiven him. It didn't make it easy to deal with, but I had no animosity toward him.

One by one, I greeted the rest. I got to meet my newest niece for the first time, since she had been born while I was gone. I didn't get to hold her right then, as her mother was wearing her in a sling, but I looked forward to it. I was relieved when we got my bags from the luggage claim and climbed into our separate cars. Coming home, even to a loving family, when I wasn't expecting to be home so soon, was a little overwhelming.

We went out for dinner on our way home. I didn't talk much, instead listened as my siblings filled me in on all that had been happening. Adam had gotten lasik and no longer had to wear glasses; my older sister, Rachel had gotten the job she'd wanted as a social worker. I had a new sister-in-law because Carson had gotten married only a month earlier. Lucas and Amanda had graduated high school. Of course, I'd heard about all this in the emails that Mom had sent me every week, but it was nice to hear it from them.

As soon as we got home, I carried my two bags down to my room and collapsed on my bed, grateful that my parents had never gotten around to emptying it into a guest room like they did with my siblings'. I was asleep within minutes.

The next day, I set an appointment with my family doctor and started taking anti-depressants. Arriving home from the pharmacy, I stared blankly at the pill in my hand. Could this little thing do it? Make me normal? Get rid of the anger and rage that threatened me daily? Make my depression disappear? It seemed like so much responsibility to place on a small purple pill. I didn't believe it could be done. I had lived with the emotional turmoil for so long that I couldn't believe it was possible. To accept the possibility of relief almost seemed to negate all the suffering I had been through. Could it truly be this easy? If so, why hadn't anyone thought to give me this chance before? Why had they been so insistent to throw faith in my face, telling me that I could be happy if I just prayed and asked God to make me so? Why couldn't someone have pointed out before, like President Hansen finally had, that God helped inspire men to make this miracle pill so that I could be normal? Why had I suffered pointlessly for so long?

I started to cry, relief and anguish mixing together to create yet another cocktail of emotions that I wasn't sure how to deal with. I filled my mouth with water and dropped the pill in, then went to lie down, praying with all my heart that this pill would prove to be the miracle it promised.

A few days after coming home from my mission, one of my best friends, Lissa, showed up at my doorstep. We'd had ups and downs in our friendship, but had always made it back up. She'd gotten married while I was gone, which had caused a bit of contention because I hadn't liked the fact that she'd lived with him for years before marrying him. But in light of everything going on, I couldn't judge her. It wasn't my place. I wanted to just be her friend.

Shortly after coming home from my mission, I gave a talk in church. A lot of my family came to see me and we had a bit of a party afterward.

"So, when are you going back?"

I was starting to get a bit perturbed. I'd expected that question. But it was getting annoying. Could people just stop asking me that already? I had no idea. It depended on a lot of things. What I didn't want to tell anyone, however, was that I didn't want to go back. They were all waiting for me to suddenly be happy and head back to my mission, but I couldn't. I didn't want to, not again. Asking me over and over again wasn't going to change my answer. But this was the first time she'd asked and had no way to know why I was upset, so I forced myself to stay calm.

"I don't know."

My grandmother looked disappointed, but I couldn't worry about that right now. My main concern was getting better. Getting to the point where I could feel normal.

After a week or two, I began to wonder if this was what "normal" felt like. I wasn't spiraling into a depression constantly. I didn't feel like I needed to stay in bed all day. So, I figured the pills were working. But something still felt wrong.

A short time later, I switched doctors, to someone I didn't see every week at church. He added an anti-anxiety pill and the two of them together worked much better. It was more effective as a duo. I was amazed how much it calmed me down.

When I got home, I called Veronica and Liv, and I realized that Veronica was going to understand me a lot more than anyone. She'd been on medication for depression since she was eight, nearly the entire time I'd known her. Maybe she could help me come to terms with everything that was happening in my life. She did. She had grown out of the phase where she needed to mock others and had a greater confidence in herself. It helped both of us and we quickly became best friends again. She helped me as I went to a therapist. The therapy surprised a couple of my old friends, but Veronica knew I needed it. She knew that I couldn't just pile on the drugs. But with my past beliefs as they were, it wasn't too surprising that others had similar ones. I wondered if they were thinking that I was feeble minded and weak like I would have thought before. She helped me realize that I didn't really care. I didn't need to. There were a lot of things that I needed to work through. The food issues, my picky eating, and many more, but as I went, various things drug to the surface and I started feeling like I could handle things, or at least understand them. It wouldn't be easy, but for the first time, it seemed possible.

Getting home also pushed me to experiment with my diet a little. I went back to eating normal, non-gluten free, food. The first bite of a normal cinnamon roll after three years was sheer heaven. After about a month or so, I got an endoscopy to see if there were any ill effects from the gluten. I was just fine. Had it really been my gallbladder all along?

During this whole time, I had no idea what I was doing with my professional life. I stumbled into another job, which amazed me because it had never before been so easy to get a job. That made it that much harder to admit that I hated it. I tried to figure out my life, but I was still lost. I started researching on the internet for a job that sounded interesting. Something that wouldn't feel so empty.

One day, as I was wandering aimlessly around online; I remembered that one of my older sister's friends had mentioned working in Alaska for a cruise and touring company. That sounded interesting. I applied. After several anxiety-creating over-the-phone interviews, I ended up getting a job as a tour bus driver. Though I still had the job I'd found after getting home, I started learning how to drive motor-coaches. It was quite different from what I was used to, but I learned quickly. I was surprised at how happy I felt behind the wheel of that huge bus. A couple of the motor coaches needed to go back to Seattle, so I drove with my supervisors there, then I flew out to Alaska, seven months after I got home from my mission. I knew that this was where I would finally be happy. This was where life would be good. Based on how content I felt, I knew I was going to where I belonged.

Three weeks before the start of the travel season, all of our drivers arrived to study the touring routes. We all learned various details about Alaska and shared them with each other so that we'd all be knowledgeable tour guides. None of us were great at taking center stage in front of a bunch of people yet, but it was fun. We learned that our fear was okay. It was normal. As we drove around, we wouldn't be looking at anyone anyway. I learned awesomely cheesy jokes and met tons of interesting new people. Mostly I worked by myself on my bus. I was getting paid for sitting around doing practically nothing half the day, waiting to pick up the next tour. I would work fifteen-hour days without difficulty. It was wonderful.

I climbed on board my bus one morning and set about doing my pre-trip inspection. I turned the motor on and flipped on every light possible. Stepping out of the bus again, I walked around it, carefully checking to be sure that every light functioned properly. In the early morning light of Alaska, just as the sun was rising at three o'clock in the morning, was the best time to put aside all of my worries and simply focus on my job. The job I loved. And for the first time, in a really long time, I actually felt happy.

I wasn't sure when it happened. Maybe it was me trying to get off caffeine and cutting back on my Dr Pepper addiction, or something, but suddenly, all the happiness seemed to vanish. I lost my ability to feel again. I couldn't focus or even think. I couldn't do anything right. With this constant lifeless feeling lingering inside of me, I felt completely absent from the world. Life was indisputably empty. So, halfway through the season, I stopped taking my two meds, cold turkey. Logically, I knew I should talk to a doctor, but they didn't appear to know what was going on in my head any more than I did. After that everything spiraled out of control. One day, I made the last mistake. I still don't know why my brain was so muddled, but I made one final mistake and it cost me my job. I went home and cried, grateful my roommates weren't home. After crying for a while, I wrote an entry on my blog through my tears about the emptiness I was feeling. Maybe someone would read it and give me some insight.

"Ugh!" I turned off my phone before it even stopped ringing and threw it on the messy floor, probably harder than I should have. "Stop calling me!"

I was so sick of my family calling me and asking if I was "okay". Or telling me that I "should be okay". Or telling me that it was going to be okay. I decided right then that I felt horrible, I shouldn't be okay, and I didn't care if it would eventually be okay. I was not right now and I just wanted to sulk. I'd just lost the one job that ever made me happy. I had the right to pout in peace.

I stayed up until three in the morning, glad my roommate was out of town so I could have the apartment to myself. After watching five episodes of Ugly Betty, I finally got tired enough to lie down on my half-deflated air mattress and fall asleep.

I woke to the sun blaring in my eyes through the open window. I groaned. That was something I definitely wouldn't miss about Alaska – the constant bright light.

I checked my watch. Nine in the morning. Not a bad night's sleep. Looking at my phone I realized I'd never turned it back on again. I'd probably missed another phone call from Mom. Might as well check my messages.

I stared in shock as notifications bombed my phone. In the nine hours that it had been off, which had been overnight, I'd missed five calls and seven text messages. Three from my mom, one from my dad, and one from Rachel. I had four messages from my brother begging me to call Mom and saying Mom was worried, one from Rachel telling me to call Mom and that she was worried, and one from my dad asking me where I was and to call Mom as soon as possible.

"What the heck?" I spoke aloud. I couldn't understand why they were all freaking out. The thought struck me that maybe something had happened to one of them. Dialing as fast as I could, I called home.

"Hello?"

"Dad, what happened? Is everyone alright? What's with all the messages?"

I heard my dad cover the phone with his hand and say that I was on the phone. A few moments later, my mom picked up. She had obviously grabbed a different phone because I could still hear my dad's soft breathing.

"Julie Ann, are you okay?"

"Yeah, why wouldn't I be? You guys scared me with all the messages, what happened?"

My dad spoke up calmly. "Elena read your blog entry and called us. She said it was a suicide note. When you didn't answer any of our calls, we thought you'd killed yourself."

A proverbial knife stabbed through my chest and I fell onto the couch, tears bursting from my eyes. My parents thought I'd killed myself. My parents, the people who were supposed to know me better than anyone in the world, actually thought I was capable of that. Anger flared inside me. I know my aunt meant well, and that she'd seen a lot in her job as a social worker, but how dare she? How dare she scare my parents, and over something I would never even consider?

I attempted to keep my voice calm, but I knew I was unsuccessful. "You what? How could you. . . why would you. . . are you serious?"

"You were so upset about losing your job and your blog post was about leaving and never coming back."

"Yeah, driving somewhere and losing myself in the drive, because that's what I'd like to do. Literally drive somewhere. I would never kill myself. Do you understand me? Never."

I was now pacing back and forth across the small living room. They thought I'd killed myself. They thought I'd killed myself. I was pretty sure the knife had migrated to my lungs now because I was having a hard time breathing. I wanted to scream. I wanted to shake my parents until they understood that I would never do something like that and how much it hurt that they could even think it a possibility.

"You can't blame us for being concerned."

I had to end this call. I couldn't talk to them right now. I couldn't talk to people who thought me capable of ruining not only my life, but my very existence. Suicide had never even crossed my mind. I had only lost my job. Yes, I'd loved that job, but it was still just a job. I couldn't say that I'd never contemplated my death before, but I'd always known that it wasn't an option. Life may have been hard, but death would be a hell of a lot worse with suicide hanging over my head. Literally.

"You know what? I'll call you back later. I can't do this right now."

I hung up before either of them could say anything. I stared at the blank wall in front of me for a few moments, barely keeping myself from throwing my phone against it. The pain I was feeling was deep.

Then I dialed Veronica's number. She'd understand.

She answered after a few rings.

"Hey, what's up?"

"My parents think I killed myself."

"What?" She sounded completely baffled. That was the response I was hoping for. "Why would they think that?"

"Apparently, my aunt read my blog entry I wrote last night and decided it was a suicide note."

"What?" She responded as if I'd just informed her that the sky was now fuchsia.

I quickly recounted my phone call with my parents, including the invisible knife that was still lodged in my ribs.

"But you just lost your job. Yeah, that sucks, but it's just a job."

"I know!" This was why I called her. Because she understood me even when my parents didn't. "I loved that job. It was an amazing job and I absolutely hate that I lost it. But suicide? Really? I never thought about it. I've been trying to figure out how to move on with my life, not end it."

"Yeah, that's. . . no. What?"

"I had turned my phone off so that I could sleep, because, hey! That's what I do! And they kept calling me. And texting me. And all-around freaking out. And I was sleeping.

Even after I called you yesterday, they still kept calling. I got sick of it and turned my phone off. Apparently, that was the wrong thing to do, because when you don't answer your phone in the middle of the night, your parents think you killed yourself." My voice took on a sarcastic tone. "Good to know, note that away."

Rationally, I knew that wasn't all there was to it, but my brain had hit the point beyond reason, and even as strong as my Vulcan-like abilities were, logic and emotion had become the same thing. It would take several more years before I would understand my parents' reaction.

"And they really thought you killed yourself." I could tell Veronica was still trying to wrap her head around the fact that someone would think that was a possibility and the knife pulled out a little. At least there was someone who understood me.

"Yeah." My voice lost that anger and moved into pain. The tears started gushing again. "They really did."

"I'm sorry J. That sucks rocks." The sympathy in her voice made my tears flow harder, but, somehow, it felt therapeutic this time.

I stood there, phone in hand, staring up at the ceiling as tears streamed down my cheeks, likely soaking my phone. I couldn't say anything and yet Veronica seemed to understand. Silence reigned for a few minutes until I found my voice again.

"Thanks, Veronica. I needed that."

"Anytime sweetie. Let me know if you need anything. I'm hugging you right now."

I could almost feel her arms around me and I silently thanked God for our friendship. I didn't know where I would be without her. I didn't want to think about it.

"I'll talk to you later."

"Love ya, J."

I breathed deeply. "I know. Love you too."

We both hung up and I sat down on the couch again. Once again, grateful that no one else was home, I cried myself to sleep.

All of my family was, what I considered, unfeeling about everything. They didn't understand the deeper problem. They brushed it off, saying that I was too good for that job anyway. The job wasn't the issue, I was a screw-up. Pure and simple. I felt it. All of those blazing emotions - all of that bitterness, sorrow, and horrible anger - came rushing back in. I seethed, yet somehow it was better than before. That numbness, the absolute lack of feeling, was worse than this lack of control. Having feelings, no matter how horrible, was better than a drug induced 'chemical lobotomy'. It took a while for my feelings to level out to a near controllable state.

My mind and body took some time to adapt to the sudden med stop. I'd lost another job and once again, I tanked. I proceeded home knowing I was somehow incapable of doing anything. A useless blob. The pain was overwhelming.

I arrived home and found yet another job. Of course, I hated it. After finally finding my dream job, working elsewhere was absolute torture. I was cleaning other people's houses, scrubbing their toilets, and mopping their filthy floors. The boredom was visceral. While I was good at it, this just didn't compare and I couldn't stand the idea of doing this forever. I started looking around again for other options—applying for jobs and looking at colleges. I put my info out there anywhere I could.

The boredom oozed out of me and into the spotless bathroom sink in front of me. I could almost feel it filling up the area around me. I'd only been doing this job for a month and already I was ready to quit, even though I really needed this job. Cleaning other people's houses? I didn't even like to clean my own house. And I was cleaning for a living. The only upside was that it was such mindless work that it gave me plenty of time to think. Except that right now, the only thing I could think of was how incredibly bored I felt.

I'd been home for two months. I was stagnant. I needed to get out and do something. Something that didn't make me feel so restless. Something that wasn't cleaning other people's houses.

I wiped a streak off the mirror. What could I do though? Sometimes it felt like this was all I was good for—cleaning, doing the things that I despised. That was all I was good at. I looked around the little room. I should have taken before and after photos. This bathroom had been covered in their hair shavings, toothpaste crusts, literal crap on the walls, and pee splattered all over the floor. Even the mirror was gag-worthy and now it was fresh and beautiful. I was fantastic at this job and I hated it with a passion. I needed something else. Anything else.

My phone rang. Looking down, I saw a number I didn't recognize. Hesitantly, I answered it. As I listened, a Provo College employee told me all about the awesome programs they had. I sat down on the side of the freshly cleaned bathtub and looked around again. I couldn't stay here, doing this. The college had hooked me at the right time. I went and spent thousands and thousands of dollars for a quick degree in Medical Assisting. I wasn't sure I wanted in the first place, but it had to be better than where I was now.

Depression ruled my life, but I wasn't about to go back on that stupid pill that had made me devoid of all feeling. My best friend lost her father around this time and I couldn't even bring myself to feel any sympathy for her. I went back to faking it. It had worked before. To an extent. We were talking about my mental health one day, and she informed me that I sounded exactly like her dad. He had been diagnosed with bipolar disorder. The irritability that I'd always just taken as a bad temper was possibly a symptom of mania. The productivity, but leaving projects undone all the time definitely was. Staying up all night, bursts of energy, all mania. Looking at my life, seeing it through new eyes, I could see how it was divided into two parts, mania and depression.

With this new insight, I went to my doctor again and asked for a new medication. The first drugs since Alaska, almost a year. The thought that I might have found a possible reason, bipolar disorder, gave me new hope. Maybe my lack of feeling with the other medication was because it was the wrong kind. Maybe I'd start the new meds and they would actually work. Maybe someone did understand and could actually help me. After visiting with my family doctor, I called my old therapist's office. She wasn't there anymore, but that was okay. I felt like I needed a new person anyway. Someone who didn't know where I'd been. Someone who could help me look forward.

When I first started taking lamotrigine, I went from zero to emotional. I became a ticking time bomb. I couldn't tell you how I would feel from moment to moment. I actually scared my father at one point because I began crying and didn't even know why. He couldn't figure it out and ended up sending me home from church early and avoiding me for a few days while I leveled out. I talked to a nurse and found out that this was a normal reaction to lamotrigine, at least at first. As my emotions leveled out and my brain adapted to the new med, my life did too.

My grades were suddenly amazing. The first term, when I wasn't on medication, I was somehow focusing better than normal as I had gotten mostly A's with one C, which was amazing for me. At Snow College, I'd had a 2.0. But after I got medicated, I got a 4.0 for the first time in my life. None of my classmates believed that it was my very first time. I had become known as the smart one. The one who always knew the answers. I read all the books. I knew all the material. I studied with Lissa who was studying to be a vet tech, so was learning similar phrases. I felt so good about myself when I graduated with high honors. It was my most amazing achievement that I had gotten thus far in my life. What I had overcome was incredible and I knew it.

I got my first job as a medical assistant in a dermatology clinic. I was learning how to do laser hair removal and watching surgeries. It was absolutely fascinating. I was even making new friends. It was unbelievable! I could finally focus well, which helped everything work out smoothly. Until my focus began to wane, again. I stopped remembering all the things I needed to. I forgot to have patients sign consent forms until after a procedure had already been done. A huge mistake! It was so difficult to get up in the morning that I arrived to work late multiple times. Nine months on the job and, surprise, surprise, I lost it. One of the best jobs I'd ever had, and I'd lost it.

When they realized why I'd been having these problems—that I had bipolar disorder—Human resources referred me to a psychiatrist in Salt Lake City. It was the first time I'd been to a psychiatrist. It didn't take long for her to conclude that my medication dosage was off, so she decided to increase it. I think it helped my mother, who came with me, to accept that this mental illness was real. The psychiatrist listened as both my mom and I recounted my symptoms. My mom helped describe the issues she'd seen and eventually agreed with her on the diagnosis.

This rollercoaster happened again and again, over and over, in a perpetual loop. It seemed like every time I changed my meds, it worked for a little while and then stopped again. Knowing that was normal for finding the right treatment didn't make it any easier. I was in the "guinea pig stage", where doctors have no better option but to test out a bunch of different drugs on you to see what works and what messes you up. It takes a lot of time to find the right medication and the correct dosage.

During this ordeal, I found a job, against my better judgment. I had decided that I wouldn't find another job until I was stable, but my parents decided that I couldn't live under their roof unemployed. I had to have a job. So, I found one at a party store near my home. Four months in, I was unceremoniously fired again.

I was in my car in the school parking lot when I got the call. It was my day off and I was confused as to why the store would be calling me.

"Hello?"

"Julie Ann, do you use a knife at work?"

My eyebrows furrowed. She didn't know? "Yeah. I have for a while. I use it as a box opener."

Her voice dripped with condescension. "You don't need to worry about coming back again."

I froze. Had I just been fired? "What about my stuff?"

"You can come get it when you have a moment, but it will have to be when I'm here and you can be observed." She hung up.

I stared at my phone. What had just happened? It's not like I'd ever hurt anyone with my knife. I'd simply used it to open boxes. I started crying. Why was I even surprised? It's not like I was ever given any of the chances that normal people were given. They knew I had bipolar. I snorted without humor. They probably figured it was only a matter of time, so many do, but I'd never given them any reason to believe that. Having bipolar disorder doesn't make me a ticking time bomb.

I called my friend, Liv. I was still crying when she answered.

"Hey J."

"Are you still hiring at your store?" I hiccupped through my tears.

"Yeah. Why?"

"I need a job."

"Got it. I'll set you up an interview with Laura."

Laura was Liv's sister and the manager of the necktie store they worked at. "Thanks."

I started the following Monday. Laura also had bipolar disorder, so she understood. And when the lamotrigine stopped working again, and they changed my medication to Abilify, she understood that it might be crazy for a few days. She understood that I might need a couple days off to level out on the new medication. It was a fairly new med that my doctor wasn't entirely sure about but figured we could give it a shot. I was reaching my limit on failed experiments, but I gave it another go, hoping, as always, that it would work this time.

What I Learned:

- People won't always understand what's going on with you. Friends and family are rarely hard to explain to, because they love you no matter what. But bosses are often less forgiving.

Actions You Can Take:

- A lot of people are going to say don't admit to having a mental illness when you get a job. Conceal, don't feel, that kind of thing. But I found that after I got the job, especially if I'm not fully treated, if I sit down with my supervisor or manager and just explain that this is what's going on, I'm doing ok, but I might need help occasionally; it goes a long way into helping them understand where I'm coming from. Then, if I do have a problem, they're a lot more lenient in helping me, because it didn't come out of the blue.

CHAPTER FIVE

Depression makes everything harder, but dating is even worse, especially when you know you're not worth their time. I'd had a crush on Brian all through junior high and high school, right up to my mission, but I knew I didn't deserve him. No one was going to understand what I was going through. They couldn't. So, naturally, I hid my pain; I faked it, again. With the medication that I took, it became a lot easier. I didn't always have to fake it, but dating still wasn't for me. No one would ever want me.

Eventually, I tried to convince myself that I didn't care. Dating wasn't that important. Really, it wasn't; or shouldn't be. I'd had a couple of boyfriends in the past, but none of those relationships lasted very long. Halfway because they drove me crazy, they just weren't quite right, and halfway because I would sabotage the relationship before it really started. Getting anywhere close to serious wasn't possible. I hoped it would somehow happen someday. I knew that I needed to find someone without a mental illness. Otherwise our kids would be doomed to this never-ending roller-coaster. I needed someone completely sane, but that could still understand me. It seemed I was asking the impossible.

As I became more aware of my illness, I was more open about the fact that I had bipolar and how it affected me. I was more open about what I had gone through. I started really talking about it with people. There were times that I drove people nuts. I was trying to change the world, but change is scary. To "normal" people, mental illnesses are those creepy things you see on TV. They don't understand them. Now I had become a "them."

One night I went to a single's activity for Halloween with our church group. As I waited for everyone to get to the church so we could carpool the rest of the way to the activity, I struck up a conversation with a girl friend of mine who also had bipolar disorder. We were talking about some of our experiences, how it sucked and how horrible and difficult it could be. A random guy who wasn't dressed at all for the occasion, walked up to us and joined in our conversation, informing us that he, too, had bipolar disorder. The three of us talked for a short time about how frustrating and challenging it could be. He and I clicked.

When it was time to carpool to the activity, the guy, David, drove us in his car. As he drove, I watched him. He was pretty good-looking: tall, dark, and handsome; but he was over two and a half years younger than I was. Having had bad experiences in the past with younger guys, I was almost sad. I knew nothing could come from this. I reminded myself I couldn't get involved with him; it was important for my future children that I not marry someone who also had this curse. I dismissed the thought of him from my head. We still ended up talking together the entire evening though.

I was okay with being friends with him, so when David stopped me after church meetings one Sunday and bluntly asked for my number, for a date, I was flattered and gave it to him. I figured that it didn't have to be more than a date. But it was very refreshing to have someone be straightforward and not beat around the bush. He wasn't playing a game and that was nice. I had a crush on someone else, but that didn't mean I couldn't hang out with other fun people.

I wasn't sure what David had in mind for our date, but I hoped it didn't involve too much driving. That night, snow had started coming down hard and it was pretty icy. He had mentioned something about Christmas lights.

When he arrived at my house, the snow white of his car put me a little on edge due to the storm we were about to drive in. His coat was bulky and I wondered absently if mine was as well. He unlocked my door before opening it for me. As he walked around to the driver's side, I leaned over and unlocked his door, something that Rachel had taught me years earlier. He looked at me through the window and smiled before getting in.

"Thanks," he said. He started the car, brushed the few snowflakes off his head, and turned up the heat. The air was still hot from before he'd come to the door and I put my hand next to the vent to warm it. It hadn't taken long for my ungloved hand to get cold in the icy outside air.

He turned toward me. "I'm assuming you're hungry. Do you have a favorite restaurant, or do you want to get take out and eat it on the way?"

"Actually," I stated, "my favorite restaurant does take out. Golden Corral charges you by weight."

He nodded and flipped a U-turn to go the right direction toward Golden Corral. Our conversation seemed to come easily as he drove and we made it to the restaurant quickly. It didn't take us too long to grab our food. Then we were on our way south. On the freeway. In what was becoming a blizzard. Was this even safe? I realized that his driving was making me super nervous. I couldn't see the lines very well, but he wasn't going straight, according to the edge of the road. Logically, I knew that he wasn't swerving badly, but it felt like he was all over. I focused on eating my food. I was starving! I felt bad that he couldn't eat since he was driving but did appreciate that he was at least focusing on the other cars on the road, even if he wasn't driving perfectly straight.

We made it safely to Spanish Fork and drove to the Christmas light show that he'd had in mind.

His brows furrowed. "It looks smaller than I remember."

"Maybe it's bigger on the inside?"

He grinned at the nerdy, Doctor Who reference and drove to the entrance to pay the fee. We soon realized that it wasn't bigger on the inside. It was, indeed, smaller than it used to be. We were allowed to go around twice if we wanted without paying again, but after talking it over, we decided that it wasn't worth it. We left the disappointing light show and stopped at a nearby gas station to sit while he finally ate his, now lukewarm, food.

On the way home, his driving seemed even worse. The blizzard had definitely come in and he was all over the road. The only thought that was going through my head was that it was a good thing this wouldn't go anywhere. My theory on driving made that impossible. People drive the way they live. If his driving made me nervous, how would his life be?

Maybe I felt sorry for him, but I suggested that we watch a show at my place when we got back. We picked a nerdy show that we both liked and started it up. He sat in the middle of the couch and I sat near the arm, feet up pointing toward him so he could get no ideas about cuddling. In my experience, that's what guys liked doing while watching shows and I wanted nothing to do with it. Cuddling would lead him on, thinking that I liked him, and after that driving, I couldn't.

Halfway through the show, my dad came down, since I still lived with my parents, and joined us. As awkward as it was for my dad to join us, it seemed to fit the pattern of the night.

Christmas came and went. Maybe I was feeling lonely, maybe I wanted a friend. Maybe I just wanted free dinner. I can't remember, but I agreed to a second date with David. I think maybe it was to convince him that a relationship between us wouldn't work. During that date, which was a month after the first, I informed him, in what I thought was a round-about way, that I wasn't interested in a relationship right then. I didn't want to lead him on, but I was definitely getting a distinct impression that he liked me. I, however, still had a crush on someone else.

I was going to Utah Valley University at the time, working toward my second degree, after my first one from Provo College hadn't gotten me far. We were, coincidentally, in a class together and David would then follow me to lunch with Veronica. She was confused as to why he was following me, but he said he liked hanging out with us and that he had a break between classes at that time. He told me later that he liked the conversations we had, but as he was planning on leaving for the summer for work, he still didn't think we'd have a relationship. He thought he was content being friends. I could see otherwise, but I rolled with it anyway. He wasn't asking me on more dates, so it was fine.

It didn't take long for me to realize that I might have feelings for David as well. Two months after our second date, when it became apparent that the guy I had a crush on, with no mental illness to worry about, didn't have feelings for me, I decided to give it a shot and see how it could go with David. My telling him that I hadn't wanted a relationship with him had actually backfired on me, because David liked me even more after that as he realized I wasn't going to be one of those "desperate, clingy girls." Suffice it to say, it went fast, which was weird since we had both intended to wait longer, at least a full year. I'd even said for a while that I needed to know someone for a year before I started dating them.

One Sunday evening, I laid my head on his lap and he slowly stroked my hair. In a way, I was glad that my friend, Joy, and her boyfriend, Phillip, had left because now it was just David and me downstairs. We'd already convinced all of my nieces and nephews to stay upstairs and now we were alone, watching a fun movie. Our relationship had come so far and I was trying to decide if I wanted the next step. I'd already decided that this time would be different. This time there would be no beating around the bush. No games. Just open, honest communication. So, I began.

"I'm trying to decide if I want to kiss you because I want to kiss you, or because it's been two years since I've kissed anyone."

I could hear the hesitation in his voice, but it came out strong somehow as well.

"I've been trying to decide how to bring up the fact that I wanted to kiss you too."

Well, that sealed it. I was so kissing this man. So, turning, I settled into his lap and went for it. I was excited to find that he was good at this! Deciding to take it one step further, I turned it into a make-out session. Something I said made him stop.

"Wait, this is your first kiss too?" he asked.

"No," I responded, kissing him again. Then I stopped as what he said registered. I pulled back.

"Wait, this is your first kiss?"

He looked embarrassed. "You weren't supposed to know that."

"No, I wish I'd known that earlier! I would have been a little more reserved."

He shrugged and pulled me in again. "It's fine."

If he was okay with it, then I would be too. I did wonder how he'd gotten so good at this, though. Apparently, he told me later, online tutorials had helped.

We started officially dating after only knowing each other for about five months. I was surprised at how refreshing it was to date him. To have someone who actually understood what I was going through. It was amazing! At one point, when we were dating, my Abilify ran out and my insurance wasn't working. He knew how important it was that I get more meds because he'd been there. It was that important to him as well. He paid for the prescription, which wasn't cheap. This happened on two occasions. He was always patient with me as I struggled without medication for a few days. My eyes were suddenly opened to the possibility of marrying a man who understood me, instead of one who could only try.

Very early on in our dating, I got sick. I called David from work, realizing that I wasn't going to be able to drive myself home. I was so grateful for someone who could come and get me.

He arrived after I'd thrown up in the bathroom at the store I worked in and helped me out to his car, where I immediately leaned the seat back so I was laying down. He drove carefully, and I reflected back on our first date when he'd driven so sporadically. He'd never done that since, and I was grateful.

When we arrived home, he once again helped me walk and get into the house. Soon after we got in, I rushed (as quickly as I could) to the bathroom again to vomit. As I threw up, the tightening of my stomach muscles made my bladder push out and I peed through my pants, creating a puddle on the floor.

"Great." I said aloud, trying to be quiet so David didn't hear. "That's awesome. My boyfriend is out there and I've peed myself."

"Are you okay?" I heard his voice from right outside the door.

"No," I groaned, remembering my promise to always be honest with him. "I need to change my clothes."

"I know." He said, softly. "I heard you."

"Great." I replied, sarcastically.

He helped me downstairs to my bedroom and left me to change while he went back upstairs.

It took me longer than it should have to change and head back upstairs. I slowly made my way by holding onto the wall. By the time I got to the top of the stairs, David was there, holding my arm and helping me to the couch.

"I need to clean up."

He shook his head. "I already got it. You're fine. Just relax."

I couldn't help but think about the possibility of marrying someone who would be willing to clean up when I was sick. If I got sick while pregnant, it would be very nice. I sighed and relaxed back into the couch, falling asleep quickly.

David and I went on a lot of long walks through the park and the cemetery across from my house. For some reason, it was easier to talk while walking and we really wanted to get to know each other better. It didn't take long for us to decide that we'd probably be getting married. One night, as we were out on a walk, we were opening up more than normal and he opened up about his struggles. He told me how when he was in junior high, he had attempted suicide. This was the first time I ever saw him cry. He told me how grateful he was that his mom had caught him, that he hadn't succeeded. I, of course, started crying as well. I wouldn't have ever known what I was missing or who he was. I was so, so grateful to have him. He had already blessed my life more than I could comprehend. I think I fell for him that night.

The night before Easter Sunday, we were at my house once again, watching a show and cuddling. At the end of the show, the guy joked that the girl had asked him to marry her. So, I turned to David and asked him if he would marry me. Of course, he responded yes. Five minutes later he suddenly spoke up.

"Wait, does that mean we're engaged now?"

I chuckled and looked at him. "Yes. Yes, it does."

The next day, we were at his house, talking. We both said that we had the feeling we needed to get married before October, instead of waiting as we'd planned. It needed to move up a lot. We talked to my parents and he stumbled through asking for my hand. Neither of my parents was surprised, though we'd only been officially dating a month and a half. We planned the wedding for the fifth of July, only two and a half months away. The wedding plans commenced.

After a whirlwind planning time, mixed in with lots of walks, it finally happened. The moment every girl dreams about. And I was a nervous wreck! Kneeling at the altar with him, looking into his eyes, I barely remember saying yes. I was so scared suddenly. Was I making the right decision? I was so scared that I wasn't going to be happy. That I wouldn't make him happy. As soon as we were declared husband and wife, though, we kissed across the altar and my worried feelings dissipated. This was right. Even if it wasn't, there wasn't anything I could do about it now.

I'd learned how to fake loving myself, but I hadn't ever learned how to truly love myself. David was always pointing out the positive things about me. Unfortunately, I didn't believe him. I didn't believe I was amazing; I couldn't believe any of that because I knew I wasn't. How could anyone think that? He was blind. One day, he would figure out what a screw-up I really was and cut his losses.

Almost a year after we got married, I got pregnant. The worry about passing my mental illness on had diminished with David's help and knowing that we'd keep an eye out for it. My children would never go through what he or I had.

What I Learned:

•

It's hard looking at your child and wondering what problems they might have. It's also hard to know you gave them that. But having a husband that understands my worries, my frustrations, and my problems has been exactly what I needed.

Actions You Can Take:

- It's worth finding someone that understands you, even if that makes you nervous. If you're married, make sure your spouse knows how they can help you. Sit down, and keep the conversation open. Ask how you can help them, and explain what they can do as well. Open communication will be your salvation.

Chapter Six

When I first got pregnant, I had no idea what to expect. I didn't know if I would be constantly sick or just fine. Would I have complications or not? I'm sure every pregnancy brings these fears, but the first one always does the worst. The most terrible fears arise and you know you have to do everything you can to keep that little baby inside of you safe. So, when my doctor told me that I needed to go off of my seemingly unimportant triglyceride medication, because the pregnancy side effects were unknown, I stopped taking it immediately. I didn't understand what I was doing to myself. Neither did my doctor.

I was blessed with less morning sickness than most, which was an amazing thing.

However, I did get antepartum and post-partum depression. Veronica acted as my doula before, during, and after the birth. She and I hung out a lot, along with Liv, and they recognized that I wasn't acting like myself. I didn't see it, but they did, which is one of the great things about having friends that know you so well. They started asking me questions.

Veronica brought up the knowledge that antepartum and postpartum depression were very real. We had discussed the fact that I would probably have postpartum de-pression, but the idea of getting depression while pregnant was new to me. So, I went back to my doctor once again and he pre-scribed me another med, escitalopram. It worked great. I went back to being able to function as my old self. I was back on track, though I hadn't made it to happy yet.

Out came the baby, our adorable little boy. Rodney. I barely got a chance to hold him before he was whisked off to the NICU, an intensive care unit for babies to be put on a CPAP to inflate his lungs. He was only there for an hour, but that did the trick. It was long enough that my heart stopped while we waited to find out if he'd be okay.

When we took him home, I breathed a sigh of relief and convinced myself that it would be all right. It didn't take much, but while the anti-depressant continued to work, it didn't take all the depression away. Also, no one had warned us that dads could get postpartum depression, too. Between David going through that, and my medication only fixing part of me, we had a very hard time. I stayed on the escitalopram, but for those first six weeks, it was very difficult. David and I had our first real argument, which was amazing considering we'd been married a year and a half. We were mad at each other for longer than we'd ever been before. For a few days, I was terrified we wouldn't make it.

David had gotten sick as well and was given a medication that interacted negatively with his bipolar medication, causing vision and balance problems. He had to go off of both for a few days while they got out of his system. That was hard as his bipolar symptoms returned. But, halfway because we're so stubborn, and partly because we took the time to take a walk and really communicate, we made it through. Communication became the most important thing in our lives as we promised to never let that happen again.

I was also very grateful to my mother-in-law for being there and staying with us through that time. She understood the difficulties of depression, as she had it too. She understood the struggles of bipolar disorder since her husband also had it. She understood me when I didn't and helped me push through in ways that I couldn't have done on my own.

Rodney had been born on Tuesday. That Saturday, on swollen feet, at three o'clock in the morning, I paced around our tiny kitchen. My mother-in-law was feeding the baby and I was freaking out. For the last few days, the swelling had been getting worse. It had gotten to the point where I could feel the crease in my ankles whenever I stood up. There was something wrong, and I had a feeling I knew what it was. Not wanting to wake my exhausted husband, but fearing what would happen if I didn't, I went into the bedroom, pulled out the equipment needed, and lightly shook him awake.

"Can you take my blood pressure?" I whispered.

With blurry eyes, he stared at me for a moment as I waited for the question to sink into his tired brain. He slowly nodded, rubbed his eyes, and reached for his glasses. I offered up the stethoscope and blood pressure cuff to him and turned on the soft light next to his bed.

With the skilled hands of a former CNA, he tightened the cuff on my upper arm and put the stethoscope against my skin. I waited with a tight chest as he read the dial.

"141 over 90." He looked at me in concern. "That's high, even for me. Let alone you."

I nodded. I'd been afraid of that. My blood pressure, normally inhumanly low, was now very high. My fears were proven, and we got dressed to head to the hospital, leaving Mom Toomey in charge of our new baby.

Four days after giving birth to Rodney, I was in the emergency room. When they took my blood pressure at check-in, it was at 150/98.

They ran a bunch of tests on me and when the doctor came back in, he had an almost happy look on his face, but I could see the concern in his eyes.

"Well, I've got good news and bad news." He set my chart down on my bed near my feet. "The good news is that you're not overreacting."

The bad news was that I was sick. Very sick. I was diagnosed with post-partum pre-eclampsia (yeah, that's a thing) and put back in a labor and delivery room. They gave me medication to lower my blood pressure while they desperately tried to find out what was causing the problem. They did an x-ray of my chest and discovered I had pneumonia, which led to another medication. They did an ultrasound of my liver and found fatty deposits on it.

The doctor in charge of me told me that they weren't sure how to help me because the cure for what I had was to have a baby. As my doctor pointed out, of course, I'd already done that. The uncertainty of it all caused my husband to break down, even while trying to be strong for me.

My mother-in-law cared for Rodney while David took care of me, and David was able to take Rodney to his bilirubin test later that same day at the hospital. Due to Rodney's abnormally high results, he ended up in the pediatric ward right below me under special light therapy. David travelled back and forth between his wife and his brand-new son, worried about both. I found out later that he cried on his mom's shoulder at least once.

While in the hospital, I pumped every three hours to try to get the milk my baby needed. I had wanted so badly to be one of those moms that would be able to feed her baby all by herself. I'd taken the classes; I'd learned all the things that I thought I needed to know. And when it came down to it, I was unable to breastfeed. "Breast is best" was what was going through my mind constantly, even knowing that formula saves lives. I wanted to breastfeed. So, I pumped while my baby was downstairs, one floor below me. I couldn't feed him. I was sick, he was sick, and the nurses wouldn't let us be near each other for a time while they desperately tried to fix me.

I couldn't breastfeed while on two of the medications that I was supposed to be on. One was the cholesterol medication, fenofibrate, that I figured I'd go back onto after breastfeeding for a while. The other was my bipolar medication, lamotrigine, which I was still on, that had mixed reviews. My neurologist said it was fine. The lactation specialist said it wasn't. I couldn't go off that one without what I knew to be horrible results on my part, so all I could do was hope and pray that it wouldn't affect my baby and that the neurologist was right.

A week later, once Rodney and I were both out of the hospital, I sat in my parents' living room. No one else was home.

I was there alone with Rodney, trying desperately to get him to accept breast milk. He refused to latch, as always. He screamed and screamed until finally, tears running down my face, I gave him a bottle. He calmed right down, eating without trouble. I sobbed. Every attempt had been unsuccessful. I felt like he hated me. Was he refusing just to spite me? Tears flowed freely, and I just held him tightly, wishing things were different.

I texted Veronica, who had been in a similar situation several years earlier. She reassured me and told me that formula was fine. My baby was going to be fine. Rodney would be great with the formula and that if it was taking that big of a toll on my mental health, I needed to just let go and stop trying to breastfeed. My mental health and my ability to care for myself needed to come first, before my stubbornness in trying to breastfeed. Rodney would be fine and I would be a better mother because of it. There were many more tears and it took a few more days for me to give in, but as soon as I made that choice, it felt right. It was time to take care of myself and let my baby eat how he wanted.

Part of taking care of myself was the fact that I needed to change my diet. While the doctors weren't sure exactly what caused the pre-eclampsia, the fatty deposits on my liver were something David and I couldn't ignore. We were sure that had something to do with it. So, I tried. I tried to eat better. I slipped up, and I tried again. But I would inevitably fall back into horrible habits of high carbs and tons of sugar. I couldn't get myself to consistently eat what I should. Even with the fear of illness, or even death, looming over me. The fear that I constantly had that I would die and leave my child motherless and my husband a widower wasn't enough. The PTSD surrounding vegetables was so strong. It took another two years for me to finally decide to see a therapist about it. It's unclear to me why it took so long for me to figure out that I needed help there too. The mistakes my parents had made are still haunting me.

They are still haunting my husband who has cried many times over my inability to get past my PTSD and eat correctly. The memory of my hospital visit loomed overhead for him.

It's the best thing in the world to have someone who understands you. Who's been through what you've been through. Who can see when you're going through a hard time and know what to do to help you.

The difficult part about that is, that it's sometimes your job to do all those things for them too. Which, of course, is fine. But it's so hard sometimes. It makes me appreciate him more because of what he does, and makes me hope that I can do the same for him. There have been times when David's medication has stopped working. And when that happens, especially when there's a young baby involved, it makes things so much harder. The mental breaks and nighttime help I'd grown accustomed to were not so readily available.

Aiden was born in November, two days before Thanksgiving. Of course, first stop was the NICU. They barely let me hold him beforehand, and that was only because I begged. He had to spend more time there than Rodney had, going back four times, and my nervousness skyrocketed. But we came home the following day with our healthy baby and sent Rodney with my parents to my grandparents' house for the holiday. We spent time together with just Aiden and were thankful for the help.

With Aiden here, the love I felt for Rodney expanded to him, but so did my fears. During the pregnancy, I stayed on the triglyceride medication, out of fear of ending up in the hospital again, like I had with Rodney. I was scared that it would be worse this time. But that didn't stop me from fearing what might happen to my baby if I stayed on a medication that made it so I couldn't breastfeed. Once again, we decided to use formula, but once again, the decision was a difficult one. Easier than the first time, but still hard. Like his brother, Aiden was a great baby and has been growing into a wonderful little boy.

The following February, David and I both got kidney stones, each within a week of each other. Mine was big enough that I had to have surgery to break it up and allow it to pass. I bounced back from that surgery and barely had any downtime at all.

A month later, David had to have the same surgery. But he didn't bounce back easily. I've never seen him cry as much as I watched him breakdown in pain after having that stone removed. His stay in the hospital was one of intense agony and little relief. Where my stay was same-day and I didn't even get a room, his stay was two days long and most of the time was spent trying to get his pain under control. Multiple commonly effective hospital pain medications hardly touched it. The next ten days while the stent was in, he stayed mostly in bed. Apparently, he was one of the unlucky ones that have stents that are far from painless.

I still had to go to work and run all of the errands on top of that, including picking up his medications and anything else he really needed. Knowing that he was doing his best didn't make it any easier on me and I cried in frustration more than once. Once again, the drugs they gave him interacted with his normal medication, which he had to take, and basically knocked him out. He was just barely coherent most of the time to go through the motions of taking care of the boys. He'd feed them both, holding the bottle without holding Aiden because he didn't trust himself to stay steady, and then put Aiden back to bed while Rodney played. He was in so much pain, even with the medication they gave him that we went back to the doctor multiple times to try to figure out why.

Everyone can only see things as their experiences allow them to. That goes for me, that goes for my husband. We evaluate each other based on those experiences. I evaluated how he should have healed from his surgery based on my experience of ease. He was amazed that I was able to be up and around and working the day after my surgery because of his pain.

It was a really hard time for us. I was used to him being able to do much more than he was doing and I was confused as to why he was in so much pain when I had just jumped out of the surgery without problems. A lot of repressed and unaddressed issues came up and for a while, it hurt our relationship. It was hard to talk through things because we weren't able to go on the walks that we were accustomed to. He could barely walk around the house, let alone around the block. So, we tried to talk in our room after the boys had gone to bed, but it was not quite as easy. For some reason, it just didn't have the same effect as talking on a walk. Our communication lagged for a while as we waited impatiently for his stent to come out.

Once we were able to take walks, and our constant communication was smooth again, we were able to work through a lot of issues. There was yelling, and crying, on both sides, but there was also love, understanding, and strengthening of each other. Our suppressed thoughts came to the surface and we were able to resolve them. They were more mine than his, as I have the tendency to push my problems to the back of my brain and hide them, until they explode out of me.

While I was pregnant with Aiden, David told me that how I reacted to his critiques was driving him crazy. Every time he would give me any kind of constructive feedback, or correct something he felt needed to be corrected, as married couples should do for each other, I would take it as an affront, as critical, as him putting me down. In my head, I would hear the words "I'm so stupid, of course, I made that mistake," and my brain didn't differentiate from his loving words and the horribly critical words saturating my mind. They were all the same. It hurt him because he didn't see me that way. He wasn't saying anything, looking back, that should have had this effect. He wasn't trying to make me cry. He couldn't say anything to me without my twisting it into a bluntly degrading insult. Once again, I was sabotaging my relationship. This wasn't fair. He loved me and would never think or say anything rude and hurtful. He was trying to build me up to the person I said I wanted to be.

The change finally happened when he challenged me, multiple times, to make a list of all the positive attributes about myself I could think of. I had a hard time coming up with more than one or two. I knew he wouldn't accept so few. So, I went on Facebook and I asked everyone to post something positive about me. I was immediately flooded with responses and overwhelmed with all these amazing things that people said about me. It was hard to believe. Even so, I wrote down everything everyone said. They didn't really mean that much to me. Some of these people barely knew me. They were kind people, trying to show love for a hopeless waste of space. Just like David and his false praise. I couldn't truly accept their compliments, even if they were being specific. I wrote the compliments down mostly to make David happy. I mean, it's what he wanted.

Then, I prayed to God. I asked Him what positive attributes I had. I was actually open and ready to hear it from Him. If any really existed, he would know them. He flooded my mind with profoundly positive attributes about myself. I had to get out my phone in the middle of the prayer to type them up on the list I'd already started. There were so many. It was extraordinary. I had never been so reassured of so many good things about myself before. This was different than hearing it from other people. Yes, I knew God loved me, but I also knew that He couldn't lie. Someone I could actually believe for a change.

I still struggle a little with thinking positively about myself, as everyone does, especially when my medication isn't working right. However, there isn't that automatic negative response to everything anymore. I never believe that my husband doesn't like me anymore or that I'm a horrible, worthless person. I never worry that, one day, he would come to believe what I "knew" then and wish he'd never married me. That night changed me forever.

What I Learned:

- Sometimes life beats you half to death and it takes a lot to bring you back. But you will come back.

- Open communication is so important. That includes with your spouse, with your therapist, and with God.

- God will not lie to you. He's your most firm supporter. He loves you and me and will do everything He can to help us make it back to Him.

Actions You Can Take:

- Go onto social media, if you're on it, and ask your friends what your good qualities are. Tell them you're going through a hard time and just need the reminder. Then write down everything that's said in a place you'll be able to access it easily.

- If you believe in God, ask him what your strengths are. Too many times we hear 'ask God what your weaknesses are so He can help you make them strengths.' But God is there to lift us up, not just point out our issues. We need to know our strengths. Making our true weakness is not seeing how amazing we are. I believe with all my heart that he will tell you. Write those down too.

Chapter Seven

Mental illnesses make relationships hard. They make everything difficult. What they make the very trickiest, however, is being a mom. There are days when I totally rock everything and go to bed feeling so accomplished that I'm shocked. Then there are days when I want to shake my children so hard they stop doing whatever they're doing. Fortunately, with my medication, I've been able to hold in those urges. There are definitely times when I have to pass the kids off to David and take a nap, or browse social media, or something, just to calm myself down. Those times are, happily, few and far between, but they definitely happen.

I love being a mom. I love it more than I actually ever thought possible. It's one of my favorite things. One of the only things that helped my postpartum depression either time was cuddling my newborn. I cherished the time I had with my babies in the middle of the night, just staring at them as they ate. I love the snuggles, the hugs, the "I wuv you"s. They bring light to my world.

There are so many days when I look at my children and wonder, "how will *I* mess *them* up?" I wonder what *I'll* do wrong. I know what my parents did wrong with me. They did their best, I know that. So even doing my best, what am I going to screw up?

I wonder, however, if my bipolar doesn't help me with that. Because I wasn't expecting much of myself going into being a mother, I don't feel the "mom-guilt" that I see so many complain about. I worry what I'll do wrong, but I don't dwell when I do make a mistake. I just vow to do better next time.

Twenty-two months after Rodney was born, Aiden came along. The love I felt for

Rodney expanded to Aiden, but so did the fears. During the pregnancy, I stayed on the triglyceride medication, out of fear of accidentally killing myself if I didn't. But that didn't stop me from fearing what might happen to my baby if I stayed on a medication that made it so I couldn't breastfeed. Once again, we decided to use formula, but once again, the decision was a difficult one. Easier than the first time, but still hard. Like his brother, Aiden was a great baby and has been growing into a wonderful little boy.

I wonder how I was worthy of having such amazing children. And they are. They are absolutely incredible children. I don't know many kids better behaved than mine. I don't know how I got that blessing, but I got it. I love it. I'm so thankful for it. But I worry, like I said, and as all parents do, I'm sure, that I'll screw up. That I'll miss something fundamental and mess my children up so badly that they can't recover. Logically, it's unlikely. What could I possibly do, as long as I'm trying my hardest, that would screw them up that badly? How much power do I think I really have?

But every mom fears the worst. Every mom lays up at night wondering how in the world she could possibly teach these kids the way she needs to. Having a mental illness doesn't make me unique in that concept. But having a mental illness does, I believe, make it worse. My bipolar and anxiety make me wonder when they'll develop the same symptoms as me. When will my oldest son hurt my younger son without being able to stop himself? Will I be able to stop him first? Will I get him medication before he goes the way of his father and tries to kill himself? Will I be there for him as my mother-in-law was for David? Will someone else? I'm sure a normal mother feels these fears, but there are days when they overwhelm me with self-doubt and terror. How could God give me these children? How could he trust me *that* much?

But he did. He does. And that knowledge and reassurance brings the terror down to an almost manageable level. If I take my medication.

Which, of course, brings me to my greatest fear of all, oddly enough. What happens if my medication stops working or I'm unable to get it for whatever reason? What if I move (as I have done recently) and my insurance stops? My greatest fear is that my mistakes will somehow impact my children in too many negative ways. How many times have I lost my temper and yelled at my two-year-old? What long lasting effects will that have? How would it be worse if I didn't have my medication? Fortunately, I have my husband and with his help, it will be fine. God is also on my side. But my anxiety rules me sometimes. Like when driving at night.

My fingers and knuckles turned white as the blood was unable to get to them. I was gripping the steering wheel so firmly that I could feel the muscle in my forearm getting tight and aching. It didn't matter. There was nothing that would stop me from holding onto that steering wheel.

Even telling myself that this rigid of a grip was actually less safe. Telling myself that I was a good driver and that the difference between night and day wasn't that much when it came to driving changed nothing. My fingers gripped that steering wheel as if it were the only thing saving me and my children from the horrifying death that my brain had somehow decided would befall us in this hour and a half trip.

"At least if the kids are asleep they'd not feel anything when you go careening to your death."

I shook my head and tried to shove the thought from my brain. We weren't going to die. I wasn't going to die. The kids would be fine.

"No. I'll just be maimed or David will die."

Just then David, who was driving the moving truck in front of me, went under an overpass and my fingers, already too tense, tightened. They had every time. Even knowing that his truck was plenty short enough to fit under every overpass we came to, I still saw in my mind's eye the image of his truck hitting the bottom and him dying. I'd be all alone. I couldn't do this alone.

"He'll die and leave me alone and then what will I do?"

I concentrated on the tail lights in front of me, watching everything that David did, wishing that I could simply will this anxiety away. It had never been this bad before.

I grabbed the radio with one hand and consciously loosened the other from the steering wheel. I needed medication for this thing. I shook my head. First thing once we get to Texas, I told myself.

"I need to talk. This anxiety is killing me, honey."

I could hear the soft smile in David's voice. "We'll be fine. Nothing's going to happen. What do you want to talk about?"

I frowned. "No idea. I just need something. We've still got forty-five minutes left!"

David started babbling on about the book he was listening to and I half listened. I couldn't concentrate, but it was helping.

We only talked for about five minutes before we both ran out of things to say. I kept looking in the backseat with the rearview mirror to reassure me that the kids were there.

"Are they breathing?"

I groaned at the thought. Now that was going to worry me the whole way to the hotel. I couldn't tell if they were or not in the dark. Even in the daytime that would have been difficult. How had my anxiety gotten this bad?

With only fifteen minutes left, I started trying to convince myself that I was simply driving home from work after a long night. I was, in a way, glad that I didn't have to worry about being tired. The adrenaline pulsing through my blood made it so that I didn't need any caffeine. I talked to myself the entire way to the hotel, glad we were so close, and literally counting down the minutes until I could stop driving. I could feel the emotional breakdown bubbling up inside me, just waiting to come out once I could get to a place where I could put the car in park.

I was right. The moment we stopped and I put the car into park, the tears started to fall. David must have sensed something was coming, because it didn't take him long before he was at my door, opening it, and gathering me into his arms as much as he could while I was still belted in the seat. I sobbed on his shoulder for more than just a few minutes, but eventually, we needed to get inside and sleep.

"I need to get this fixed. That should *not* have been the scariest experience of my life!"

David nodded. "As soon as we can, honey."

I was shaking so badly that I didn't trust myself to carry anything, so David took several trips up and down stairs to get everything we needed. I appreciated the thoughtfulness of his actions and told him so. We quickly got the kids ready for bed and climbed into ours. The day caught up with me and I fell asleep quickly.

The next day was better, but it was still scary. Thankfully most of the drive was in the daytime, which made me a little less anxious. The chattering and happy noises of the kids in the background helped my nerves, as did talking to David on the radio occasionally. But I was grateful when we finally pulled up to the house and our journey was over.

Moving to Texas was my second chance at life, at happiness. So I got on a new medication, even though it might trigger a guinea pig stage. It never happened. My new prescription, Trintellix, became my saving grace. A gift from God.

What I Learned:

- Medication is so important. Therapy can do a lot, but if you are still struggling, medication can be the greatest thing ever. Without it, I'm a different person. I hate that person, and she isn't nice.

- Anxiety can be debilitating. When you are breaking down in terror, you cannot function. You have to address that issue first, then you can move on from there.

Actions You Can Take:

- Find a therapist. Go to them. Be honest. If that therapist doesn't work out, try another one. Keep trying until you find the right person. It shouldn't take you long. Therapists are amazing people! They are honestly there to help.

- If you've done all the actions in this book and are still struggling, you may need medication if you haven't already gone that route. Don't EVER feel ashamed of taking medication for a mental illness. It's a physical ailment. You wouldn't balk at blood pressure medication. Your mental illness medication is no different.

- Know you are loved. Know you are wanted here. Know you are needed.

CONCLUSION

Last night, I ate green beans! They were freshly cooked on a stove and full of flavor. I paused between bites for prayer and had to stop myself from reaching out and taking another bite. I craved them so much. Fresh, sautéed asparagus is my new favorite food, even over potatoes. I've come a long way since those days at the kitchen table, trying not to gag and paying dearly for it.

My parents and I get along well. They've acknowledged their mistake when it came to my food intake. I know that they did the best they knew how at the time. I've also come to understand the fear they felt when they thought I'd killed myself and that my anger was unfounded.

My bipolar is well-managed and no longer affects my waking and sleeping life. My anxiety levels are under control, even when driving. My PTSD surrounding food is slowly going away and I try new foods more often, though it's still hard sometimes. I'm even getting back into the medical field that I love and have gotten a job there recently.

Partly due to my understanding and my acceptance of my bipolar disorder, my father has come to acknowledge his own mental disorder. He has worked with a therapist and is doing a lot better. I put myself out there. I talk about my experiences. I don't want to help just one person though. I deeply feel the need to help as many people as possible to recognize that they can be who they want to be. That they can love themselves. That they can learn. That they can be amazing. They don't have to just live with the insanity that is mental illness. They can find the help they need. They can feel loved. They can do anything.

I want people to understand how hard it can be for some to acknowledge a mental illness. There are some in my own family that don't seem to fully understand how hard that is for me to accept my own illness. I don't think they fully understand how hard it is for my dad.

When you're dealing with depression, bipolar, anxiety, etc., it's hard to sit back and see your positive attributes. You can't do that effectively when you're being crushed by depression, drowning in your own false stupidity, flaunting how horrible and obnoxious you must be, and constantly reminding yourself that nobody likes you. It's almost impossible to allow the thought "I'm amazing" in when all of those degrading thoughts are crowding your mind. But if you can manage to reach inside yourself, outside yourself, or somewhere, and learn to appreciate you, then the depression will begin to lose its tight hold over you.

Sometimes it's going to require medication before you can get to the point where you can actually see it. That's okay. I could never have gotten to where I am today without medication and the social support from those around me. It has helped soften the destructive thoughts that were eating away inside me. When you can do that, you can overcome the seemingly impossible. You can do anything.

There are so many times when people ask "If you could do anything differently with your life, what would you change?" When I stop and really think about it, though, I realize that I wouldn't change a thing. Without all the hardships, the pain, the happiness, sorrow, and craziness I've gone through, I wouldn't be who I am today. I wouldn't now recognize how worthwhile my life is. Those things have shaped my life for the better.

Some people can get by using only supplements. In my case and for many others, supplements aren't enough. The urge to stop my meds lingers constantly, but when

I forget to take them, I get a nasty reminder of my past. I don't like being dependent on a drug. I hope that someday there is some sort of cure for this but, until then, I am grateful for what I do have—a life filled with love, understanding, and dotted with joy and contentment. I will never go back.

We need to raise awareness, to spread the word. We need to realize that mental illness is a real physiological thing. All the stigmas that surround it only make it worse. Depression isn't just feeling sad. Bipolar disorder isn't changing your mind or being moody. The person with a mental illness isn't defined by it. Please share this message. Be the light in someone else's nightmare.

Moving forward in my life, as my children get older and we watch for mental illness, I intend to take them to get a mental checkup every year. Most people get physicals every year; that's encouraged, almost pushed by society. It's good to have a healthy body. However, no one ever suggests "mentals." My dream is for that to become a standard practice. For that to become a new health trend. Why doesn't society encourage us to treat the whole system? Why doesn't anyone get a check up on their brain? It's what runs the whole body. You have your computer checked for viruses, have updates put in, occasionally give it a check-up. Why not your own, innate computer? After years of hardship, my husband and I have the ability to do it for ourselves, but not everyone can.

Recognizing your feelings and accepting yourself is the first step to a fulfilled life. Whatever you're feeling, positive or negative, face it with a newfound understanding that you're not alone, you are worth love and respect, and that help is available for you. You can, like me, climb up out of the impossible pit and learn to thrive.

About the Author

Julie Ann Toomey is an author, mom, and mental wellness life coach. Her battles with bipolar disorder, anxiety, and PTSD have compelled her to raise awareness to help others who are struggling. Ten percent of the proceeds of each of her books go to a charity that coincides with her book topic, including those from her fiction novels, as those all have some sort of mental illness in them as well.

She lives in Texas with her husband, David, and their 2 adorable boys. She works in the medical field at a family practice clinic and owns a sewing business on the side with her husband. She enjoys reading, writing, but not arithmetic. Woodworking, knife throwing, and crochet are some other hobbies she has. David says she's the perfect amount of eccentric.

Even though she's been through a lot in her life, she feels it's worth it if she can reach out to someone and help them. That's her goal with the books she writes: to help change the world, one person at a time. You can connect with Julie Ann on Facebook or on her website at julieann.toomey.org.

Books by Julie Ann Toomey

Failure to Thrive – My Journey to Mental Health

***

More Than Our Yesterdays

BOOKS BY JAE TOOMEY

Deception by Magic

Trilogy
Guardian of the Prince

Resources

This QR code will take you my page of resources. Please know that you aren't alone and there is always help!

julieann.toomey.org/resources

PREVIEW FOR MORE THAN OUR YESTERDAYS

T hings seemed to change drastically as we pulled into the driveway of my in-laws' house in Texas. It was September 2018. I tried. I tried to keep going. I tried to keep up with everything. My anxiety was haunting me every second of every day; I was certain that something horrible would happen. I was convinced that the bunk bed that my husband built for the kids would collapse and they would both die. I would lay awake, waiting to hear the crash, the screams, but telling myself over and over that if David had built it, it was sturdy. He even took me into their bedroom and showed me he could stand and even jump on it; that it wouldn't collapse beneath our children. Though it helped logically, It didn't stop the irrational fears from running rampant in my mind. I tried some books. I tried to tell myself I was fine. The biggest thing I did, however, was pray.

Driving short distances was alright, mostly because I knew the area from times we visited before, but long distances were much more difficult. Anywhere I didn't know, I couldn't drive. I'd drive as far as two or three blocks to the store, but for the rest of it, I stopped driving for a while, letting David take the wheel for the foreseeable future.

Not yet having insurance in Texas yet made it impossible for me to go get professional help with my extreme anxiety. And it wasn't something my established doctor, back in Utah, could do with only a phone call. So we waited. My anxiety grew. We could still get my bipolar medication, given by my doctor in Utah.

One night in late October, only a month and a half after we'd moved, as David drove home from a restaurant we had gone to with his family, I got a phone call from my best friend's estranged husband. He left a message, as I didn't answer in time. At first, I thought it was Lissa, just using his phone to call me. Odd, but not completely out of the question. Then I heard the message.

It was from Kyle, her husband, urging me to call him back as soon as possible. A knot formed in my stomach. Even while driving to Texas, my anxiety had never ramped up this much. As soon as I heard those words, I knew what had happened.

"Relax," I told myself. *"It's fine."*

My stomach didn't believe my brain. I'm not sure even my brain believed my brain.

"Maybe she's missing." I tried to call Kyle on Facebook messenger.

"Maybe she's in the hospital." He didn't answer.

The butterflies in my stomach turned into angry bees, swarming in ways I'd never experienced before. I typed in the phone number he gave me. We pulled up to the house, and I got out of the car.

"Maybe I'm wrong." He answered his phone.

"This is Kyle."

"Kyle, this is Julie Ann." I responded to his tired tone.

"Julie Ann. Ali is. . . no longer alive."

I couldn't breathe. "Please tell me she didn't kill herself."

"She. . . did." He responded to my plea.

I fell to my knees outside the car and sobbed. I mean, I ugly cried. I'd never had someone so close to me die before, and I didn't know what to feel. The suddenness and manner of death hit me like a ton of bricks. It felt like my personality was split in two, one side logical, the other emotional. One side crying, the other going over logistics. After I got off the phone and into the house, I immediately wrote down my experience, knowing if I could get it on paper, it would be easier to process.